THE LITERATI

JUSTIN FLEMING

AFTER MOLIÈRE'S
LES FEMMES SAVANTES

CURRENCY PRESS
SYDNEY

GRIFFIN
THEATRE
COMPANY

CURRENCY PLAYS

First published in 2016
by Currency Press Pty Ltd,
PO Box 2287, Strawberry Hills, NSW, 2012, Australia
enquiries@currency.com.au
www.currency.com.au

in association with Griffin Theatre Company

Copyright: The Literati © Justin Fleming, 2015, 2016.

COPYING FOR EDUCATIONAL PURPOSES
The Australian *Copyright Act 1968* (Act) allows a maximum of one chapter or 10% of this book, whichever is the greater, to be copied by any educational institution for its educational purposes provided that that educational institution (or the body that administers it) has given a remuneration notice to Copyright Agency Limited (CAL) under the Act.
For details of the CAL licence for educational institutions contact CAL, 11/66 Goulburn Street, Sydney, NSW, 2000; tel: within Australia 1800 066 844 toll free; outside Australia 61 2 9394 7600; fax: 61 2 9394 7601; email: info@copyright.com.au

COPYING FOR OTHER PURPOSES
Except as permitted under the Act, for example a fair dealing for the purposes of study, research, criticism or review, no part of this book may be reproduced, stored in a retrieval system, or transmitted in any form or by any means without prior written permission. All enquiries should be made to the publisher at the address above.

Any performance or public reading of *The Literati* is forbidden unless a licence has been received from the author or the author's agent. The purchase of this book in no way gives the purchaser the right to perform the play in public, whether by means of a staged production or a reading. All applications for public performance should be addressed to Smith & Jones Management, 8th floor, 10-14 Waterloo Street, Surry Hills NSW 2010, Australia; ph: +612 9213 9612; email: david@smithandjonesmgt.com.au

Cataloguing-in-publication data for this title is available from the National Library of Australia website: www.nla.gov.au

Typeset by Dean Nottle for Currency Press.
Cover design by RE:.
Cover photo shows Kate Mulvany. Photography by Brett Boardman.

Currency Press acknowledges the Traditional Owners of the Country on which we live and work. We pay our respects to all Aboriginal and Torres Strait Islander Elders, past and present.

Contents

THE LITERATI

Act One	1
Act Two	12
Act Three	39
Act Four	62
Act Five	78

Theatre Program at the end of the playtext

The Literati was first produced by Griffin Theatre Company and Bell Shakespeare at the SBW Stables Theatre, Sydney, on 27 May 2016, with the following cast:

PHILOMENA / VADIUS	Caroline Brazier
TRISTAN TOSSER	Gareth Davies
AMANDA	Kate Mulvany
CHRISTOPHER / CLINTON	Jamie Oxenbould
JULIET / MARTINA	Miranda Tapsell

Director, Lee Lewis
Co-Composers and Sound Designers, Max Lambert and Roger Lock
Designer, Sophie Fletcher
Lighting Designer, Verity Hampson
Stage Manager, Charlotte Barrett

The author wishes to thank John Azarias, Patricia Azarias, Mike Baird, John Bell, Bell Shakespeare Company, Botanic Gardens and Centennial Parklands, Fae Brauer, Melanie Carolan, Currency Press, Andrea Demetriades, Gale Edwards, Kim Ellis, Peter Evans, Claire Grady, Griffin Theatre Company, Will Harvey, Lee Lewis, The Lysicrates Foundation, Dominic Perrottet, Lane Pitcher, Morgan Powell, Fiona Press, David Stewart, Rob Stokes, Christopher Stollery and Ben Winspear.

For Fiona Press, in loving memory of The Prince.

CHARACTERS

CHRISTOPHER, a decent middle-class man
PHILOMENA, his wife
AMANDA, their elder daughter
JULIET, their younger daughter
CLINTON, Juliet's lover
TRISTAN TOSSER, a poet
DOCTOR ATHÉNAÏS VADIUS, a female scholar
MARTINA, a kitchen maid
ATTORNEY, female

SETTING

A house in Paris.

PLAYWRIGHT'S NOTES

In this version, the names of the characters are also 'translated' so as to be more Anglophonic.

A note on Vadius: In this version, Vadius is female, and I have drawn upon Francoise Athénaïs, marquise of Montespan (1641–1707), a well-educated woman of famous and considerable wit. She was referred to usually as 'Athénaïs' (the Greek goddess of Wisdom). She was chief mistress of King Louis XIV of France, and was a good friend to Molière whom she allowed to use her apartments to rehearse. In 'Love and Louis XIV', Antonia Fraser describes her as 'astonishingly beautiful, at once sexy and imperious. This voluptuousness makes plausible at least one story by which Louis plotted to spy on her at her bath disguised as a servant; awestruck, he gave away his presence, at which Athénaïs laughingly dropped her towel.'

A note on the rhyme scheme: Though Molière used rhyming couplets throughout, his audience was used to them, and in French they have less intensity. For variety's sake, and to give themes their breathing space, in scenes on lofty pretentiousness, the rhyming couplets are used (AABB). When the subject is love, the rhymes are on alternate lines (ABAB). And for wisdom and true scholarship, the rhymes fall on the first and fourth lines, and the second and third lines (ABBA).

– JF

This play went to press before the end of rehearsals and may differ from the play as performed.

ACT ONE

SCENE ONE

AMANDA, JULIET.

AMANDA:
What? You mean you'd give up your cool and carefree life
As a happy single girl, to be a bitter and twisted wife?
Why risk everything on marriage? You'd be better off dead.
Can such a gross little plan really have entered your head?
JULIET:
Yes.
AMANDA:
Who'd have thought, my dear sister, that the simple word 'Yes'
Could fill the heart with utter disgust and absolute awfulness?
JULIET:
Okay: what is it about marriage itself that puts you in a bind?
Surely it's a natural goal to leave maidenhood behind?
AMANDA:
Oh my God! Get real!
JULIET:
                What?
AMANDA:
                        I mean, get a grip, Janet.
JULIET:
My name's not Janet.
AMANDA:
                Juliet—you're on some other planet!
Doesn't it make you shudder? Dear sister, come to your senses!
Could you ever resign your heart to such hideous consequences?
JULIET:
The consequences of 'marriage', Amanda, as far as I can tell,
Are a husband, some children and a home in which to dwell.

AMANDA:
> For heaven's sake! So being in a straightjacket appeals to you?

JULIET:
> One has to ask at my age, if there's anything better to do
> Than attach yourself to a husband, for whose company you yearn,
> A man who loves you madly, and you love in return?
> For a couple so well-matched, surely this bond is enchanting?

AMANDA:
> You've sunk to a new low there. My God, girl, you're ranting.
> The world's a major stage, and you settle for a minor role,
> Locking yourself away in some domestic little hole,
> Never to glimpse life's pleasures, becoming an emotional cripple,
> With an idol for a husband and a brat on every nipple.
> It's not for you, those basic chores, cleaning, washing, dusting:
> Leave all that to people who are vulgar and disgusting.
> Hold in contempt the material world, that sense of daily grind,
> And devote yourself, as I do, entirely to things of the mind.
> You have our mother for a role model, so cultured and discerning,
> Who is hailed by the literati as a woman of higher learning,
> So prove that you're her daughter! Do try it! It worked for me.
> Aspire to the dazzling heights which illuminate our family;
> Render yourself learnèd! And check out science and art;
> Feel the power that a love of study pumps into the heart;
> Forget being a grovelling slave, where a man's rules are the norm;
> Marry yourself to philosophy, and take the world by storm!
> Taste the beautiful fires, the music of the spheres,
> And live life's every moment in the realm of perfect ideas.

JULIET:
> Live your life in the stars, let your genius take flight,
> Ascend the highest heaven of literature and light.
> But as for me, I'll settle for marriage and all of its charms;
> Some of us are born with wings, the rest of us have arms.
> So in our separate lives, in one way or another,
> Both of us will do our best to emulate our mother.
> You will be that side of her up there with the high-fliers,
> While I will be her common sense with more mundane desires;

You will delve into clever books and enjoy scholarly chatter
And I'll take care, my sister, of the little things that matter.

AMANDA:
I'm sorry, Jules, but that is just a load of utter twaddle;
When you decide to imitate the life of your role model,
You aim to resemble her finer points—her talents and her wits,
You don't model yourself on how the woman coughs and spits.

JULIET:
But you would not be here, with all of your boastful pride,
If mother had only pursued her intellectual side;
How fortunate that her flair for the analytical and the quizzical
Occasionally took a break, so she could focus on the physical.
For heaven's sake, out of fairness, concede that I might be right
To enjoy those mortal pleasures which brought you into the light.

AMANDA:
Well, I see that your so-called mind is incapable of disinfection,
As you insist with mule-headed madness that marriage is perfection.
But might we know, if you'd be so good, who your husband will be?
I mean, you haven't set your narrow sights on Clinton, surely?

JULIET:
Why shouldn't I? Is Clint unworthy? Is he somehow a bad plan?

AMANDA:
No. But it's a pretty low act to steal someone else's man,
As it's no secret that Clinton always had the hots for *me*.

JULIET:
Yes, but all his advances just appealed to your vanity,
As you never let him kiss you or do anything remotely tender,
And you made it clear a wedding was simply not on the agenda.
Philosophy was your lover, as you announced without pretence;
You felt nothing for Clint, so how can you now take offence?

AMANDA:
Just because I reject *as husband* a man who's clearly desirous
Doesn't mean he shouldn't remain on the queue of my admirers.

JULIET:
I never tried to stop him from worshipping your perfection,
But when you gave him the flick, I accepted his affection.

AMANDA:
>But an offer of love from a jilted man is risky, haven't you found?
>Can you believe in passion thrust at you on the rebound?
>And are you sure that the wild desire he had for me is dead?

JULIET:
>Yes, I am, Amanda, because that's exactly what he said.

AMANDA:
>Believe that, you'd believe anything; you're so easy to deceive.
>He's fooling himself that he left me for you; my dear, you are naïve.

JULIET:
>One of us is wrong, and the other is clearly right;
>Here he comes, right on cue, to shed much-needed light.

SCENE TWO

CLINTON, AMANDA, JULIET.

JULIET:
>Clint, we've got a problem here; maybe you might help us out?
>My sister just threw me the line that, when push comes to shove,
>The content of your heart is a matter for serious doubt;
>So please explain: is it she or I who is entitled to your love?

AMANDA:
>No, no—I'm not going to be part of some rigorous interrogation
>By subjecting someone's private feelings to public expression;
>I know how to treat people, and they hate the situation
>Where they have to make, face to face, an embarrassing confession.

CLINTON:
>Tell me which part of this you simply don't get:
>Every nerve in my body, every feeling in my heart
>And every thought of love I have is for adorable Juliet.
>I was attracted to you, sure, right from the very start:
>You swept me off my feet and opened my heart like a surgeon,
>Which was ample proof, I'd say, that your arrow had hit its target;
>I had a roaring flame for you, but you're as tough as an Amish virgin,
>And in your eyes, as a conquest, I wasn't sufficiently upmarket.

He looks at JULIET.

My dream of someone more human came true when I saw these eyes,
In them was something precious, which I knew I'd value forever;
They had a healing kindness, with no deception or lies,
She welcomed what you rejected, was wise where you were clever.
So rare is her goodness that I was totally captured
And until the day I die, I never want to be set free,
So read my lips, Mandy: with you I'm no longer enraptured,
And don't you even think about trying to rekindle me.

AMANDA:
In your dreams.

JULIET:
Lighten up, Mandy. What happened to your eloquent notion
Of superior reason to moderate the animal within,
And control the bridle to keep a check on the forces of raw emotion?

AMANDA:
As you don't practise what you preach, your words wear pretty thin.
You choose the love offered you, without consulting either parent;
They have authority over your heart; you must have their permission;
Yet you love a man they haven't approved, which a daughter daren't,
And bypassing their consent to marry is a criminal omission.

JULIET:
Clint, will you take steps to obtain my parents' consent,
To ensure that my wishes are given full and legitimate force;
Then I'll be given a license to love you, without criminal intent.

CLINTON:
I'll work with all my heart to achieve all that, of course.
I was only waiting for you to give me the green light.

AMANDA:
>I detect an element of triumph in your facial expression
>As if you imagine your happiness will flood me with spite.

JULIET:
>Me? Not at all. What on earth gave you that impression?
>I know that dispassionate analysis is uppermost in your mind
>And that because of all the principles afforded by higher learning,
>You're way beyond spite or envy, which are gross and unrefined;
>In fact, far from believing that the lady's not for turning,
>I actually think you can help me, by condescending to our plane
>And giving our relationship your weighty vote of support,
>Helping to plan our happy day, choosing flowers and champagne;
>I'm recruiting you, dear sister, and the first thing you ought …

AMANDA:
>You must be joking, Juliet! Are you out of your tiny mind?
>You're being awfully cocky about a lover I flung at you!

CLINTON:
>Look—

JULIET:
>   So he was a reject, to whom you once were inclined,
>And if your eyes are an indication, a love you'd gladly renew.
>You'd happily take him back if it meant grovelling at his feet!

AMANDA:
>I will not plunge to your level to dignify that observation,
>As I find this entire discourse appallingly indiscreet.

JULIET:
>How very wise of you to show unprecedented moderation.

SCENE THREE

CLINTON, JULIET.

JULIET:
>Well, your sincere confession really knocked her for six.

CLINTON:
>Yeah, well she deserved it; she's as subtle as a ton of bricks.
>Anyway, as soon as possible, I'll have a chat with your father.
>[*Going*] So I've gotta zip—

ACT ONE

JULIET:
> ...For a more certain outcome, I would rather
> You try to win over my mother, because she's the chief of state;
> Father will agree to anything, so his decisions don't carry much weight.
> And despite what happened just now, do try to placate my sister,
> She might actually be nice to you, if you put a bandaid on her blister.
> If you find her bitter and flat, your charm will jump-start her battery,
> Because as you know, her Achilles heel is bucketloads of flattery.

CLINTON:
> Yeah, but I really find flattery hard, because I was born sincere.
> And I like to keep it real, you know, and not put on some veneer,
> I find with clever ladies that it's sort of insulting to flirt;
> If women want to be scholars, fine; whatever lifts your skirt,
> But: the ones who treat you like fools are unbelievable shockers,
> Like they have to tell the entire world their brain is totally chockers.
> I love a truly erudite woman, without any pomp or pretence
> Who doesn't have to parade the fact that her knowledge is immense,
> She spreads her knowledge warmly, like light through a prism.
> She doesn't use gigantic words like antidisestablishmentarianism;
> Take the case of your mother: now you know that I respect her,
> But every time she opens her gob, you get a bloody lecture.
> I refuse to be a parrot who just echoes her every word,
> And the praise she heaps on her heroes is totally absurd.
> Like Tristan Tosser, for example; the man bores me to sobs;
> It drives me crazy the way your mother gets off on such knobs.
> The man's an idiot, a pedant, whose head's full of total vapour,
> Which is why all his books get pulped and end up as toilet paper.

JULIET:
> I agree; Tristan's writings have no style or merit at all;
> To say he's as thick as a brick is defamatory to a wall,
> But given the great power he exerts over my mother
> It's difficult to know what to do in this predicament, other

Than force yourself to regard him with a sort of complacence;
Because in order to gain favour, a lover has to have patience
To win the hearts of everyone connected to his love.
Even wooing the family dog is not something he's above.

CLINTON:
Yes, I know, you're right, but Tristan Tosser, on the whole,
Inspires a powerful loathing in the very pit of my soul.
And to win his support for us, I would never agree
To praising the works of someone who is so talent-free.
It was through Tristan's writing, that I first had word of him,
Before that, I'm glad to say, I had never heard of him.
I tried to read his poems. Big mistake. They're absolute bollocks;
But it doesn't stop His Pedanticness going off on literary frolics.
The unremitting arrogance of the man is pretty breathtaking,
And his inflated self-confidence is truly groundbreaking.

JULIET:
You've got pretty good eyes to notice all that with such coherence.

CLINTON:
That's the thing: Tristan's work matches his appearance.
Before I saw him I knew he'd look as boring as his writing:
Deadly dreary, totally suss and majorly unexciting;
So I subjected my prediction to the strictest test of all:
Would I be able to pick him out at a writers' festival?
And I bet against all odds he was the man coming towards me
And sure enough that was exactly who he turned out to be.

JULIET:
You're kidding!

CLINTON:
No I'm not; I swear to God, I won the bet!
Anyway, your sister's back; I hope she's not still upset.
But please don't worry, I'll do my best one way or another
To bring out her better angel and hope she'll persuade your mother.

SCENE FOUR

CLINTON, AMANDA.

CLINTON:
  Please let me say some things a man in love needs to say,
  So that in these happy days when my heart is filled with awe,
  You might graciously make an attempt to see things my way …
AMANDA:
  That was quite a performance that you put on before,
  Pretending not to be in the ranks of my devotees.
  But you're right to hide your love for me; just let it hunger in
      silence,
  Though I can tell even now, that you've gone all weak at the knees.
  He goes to speak.
  To try and put it in words is a form of linguistic violence.
  Love me, sigh for me, burn for my dangerous touch,
  But I have no space in my life for your hot infatuation,
  So don't permit your lips ever to name it as such,
  Instead, you must confine your love to mute adoration.
CLINTON:
  Amanda, there's no cause at all for concern of any fashion;
  I meant it when I said that Jules is the love of my life,
  And I come to you to beg you to show a little compassion
  And to second my proposal to make your sister my wife.
AMANDA:
  Oh, this has got to be the most roundabout form of semantics,
  So subtle is your pretence, that it deserves the highest praise;
  One reads in novels the amazing deception employed by
      romantics,
  But yours is surely the boldest and most ingenious of displays.
CLINTON:
  Actually, no it isn't. What I'm saying is not fabrication,
  It's a completely accurate statement of what's here in my soul.
  Destiny has decided, with unshakeable determination

To attach me to beautiful Juliet; and that is my only goal.
Jules holds my heart in the grip of her perfection
And getting married to her is the best thing I'll ever do.
Now, you carry great influence to nudge things in that direction,
And you could advance all my wishes if only you'd agree to.

AMANDA:
I can see very clearly where your little request is leading;
I get it: you've switched our names so as to live a fantasy life;
It's a very clever device, but has little hope of succeeding:
You want to marry *her*, but in your head, *I'm* your wife.

CLINTON:
That is so warped! What's the point of all this confusion?
You're inventing a situation that simply will never arise!

AMANDA:
My God! *I'm* inventing?! It's *you* who's under an illusion!
You say you don't love me, yet you look at me with bedroom eyes!
So let me see if I understand the rules of your little fiction:
Under this subtle scheme, though it's Juliet you claim to love,
You resolve your secret ecstasy by a convenient contradiction:
That whenever you make love to her, it's me you are thinking of.

CLINTON:
What?

AMANDA:
    Goodbye.

CLINTON:
        You're insane.

AMANDA:
            Don't you push me, Jacko!
My customary modesty will not tolerate anything uncivil!

CLINTON:
I'll be damned if I love you! You are so totally whacko!

AMANDA:
No, no, I've heard quite enough of your nonsensical drivel.

CLINTON:
> What the hell did I see in her? How unbelievably twisted!
> And how can such a monster to sweet Juliet be sistered?
> We have to turn this negative into a definite plus
> By seeking the help of someone wise, who genuinely cares about us.

END OF ACT ONE

ACT TWO

SCENE ONE

VADIUS, CLINTON.

CLINTON:
    Who better than a true scholar to push our worthy cause?
    Doctor Athénaïs Vadius, in black, with calm voice and manner;
    An old friend of Juliet's father, there's nobody better than her:
    She's a respected learnèd woman, in letters and scientific laws.

VADIUS:
    Yes, yes, my dear Clinton, of course I will plead your case;
    Go now; I'll start with her father, and inform you of his reply.

    CLINTON *goes.*

    A young lover in a hurry cannot, on his own words, rely,
    So he needs a voice to put his thoughts at a less urgent pace.

SCENE TWO

CHRISTOPHER, VADIUS.

VADIUS:
    I trust you are well, Christopher?

CHRISTOPHER:
                              Yes, Athénaïs, and you?

VADIUS:
    Yes, yes, I have no complaints; you do know why I'm here?

CHRISTOPHER:
    Not yet, but in your own time, I'm sure you'll make that clear.
    Drink?

VADIUS:
        No, thanks, I'm fine. I wasn't sure if you knew
    About the young Clinton—you've known him for a while?

ACT TWO

CHRISTOPHER:
Indeed I certainly have; he comes here quite a lot in fact.
VADIUS:
And do you like him?
CHRISTOPHER:
Yes, I do. He has a certain grace and tact,
Keen spirits, a good heart, and he shows a bit of style.
To be honest, you don't see many people as deserving as he.
VADIUS:
Well, it's a specific request of his that brings me here today,
So I am very glad to hear all the encouraging things you say.
CHRISTOPHER:
I got to know his late father when I was in Rome, you see.
VADIUS:
All the better.
CHRISTOPHER:
A wonderful friend, and a fine gentleman too.
VADIUS:
I'm glad to hear it.
CHRISTOPHER:
Both of us were about twenty-eight or so;
We were green about the gills, and yet quite dashing, you know.
We scored a hit with the beautiful Roman women.
VADIUS:
I believe you.
CHRISTOPHER:
Yes, our famous escapades were all the talk of the town.
The Italians were quite envious.
VADIUS:
Well, they're a jealous mob, no doubt.
But let's return to the subject that we'd begun to chat about.

SCENE THREE

CHRISTOPHER, VADIUS, AMANDA.

AMANDA *appears, eavesdropping.*

VADIUS:
Clinton has made me his advocate to give you the lowdown.
His heart is greatly taken by your graceful Juliet.

CHRISTOPHER:
Really? My daughter?

VADIUS:
                      Yes, he seems to have their whole lives
   plotted,
And I have to say I have never seen a young man so besotted.

AMANDA:
No, no—I couldn't help overhearing—and I think you mustn't get
The story completely wrong; the truth is otherwise, you'll find.

CHRISTOPHER:
In what way, my dear?

AMANDA:
                  Clinton has you both misled;
The object of his desires is someone other than what he said.

VADIUS:
Is this a joke? You say it's not Juliet he has in mind?

AMANDA:
No, I assure you, it's not.

VADIUS:
                    But he told me so face to face.

AMANDA:
Ah, yes!

VADIUS:
      You see me here because he sought my intervention
To express to her father his very passionate intention.

AMANDA:
Well of course.

ACT TWO

VADIUS:
                He expressly asked me to plead his ardent case
For the earliest possible wedding.

AMANDA:
                              What a romantic conception;
I have to say this story just seems to get better and better,
Seeking permission to marry, and going so far as to set a
Date, when 'Juliet' is a codename for a cheeky deception.
It's a little game he plays, a veil, a pretext, a front
To cover up his true desires by adorning them in mystery.
I have bounteous experience of this, in my own personal history,
So I can enlighten both of you as to the nature of this little stunt.

CHRISTOPHER:
Well, if you have so much knowledge of this curious affair,
Perhaps you wouldn't mind saying who this other woman might be?

AMANDA:
I thought you'd never ask.

CHRISTOPHER:
                So who?

AMANDA:
                      Me!

VADIUS:
                      You?

AMANDA:
                      Me!

CHRISTOPHER:
                          Well!

AMANDA:
What do you mean, 'Well'?

CHRISTOPHER:
[*With a laugh*]   You're kidding, right? LOL!

AMANDA:
Why is it so surprising? You know how men look at me.
I resist them all, of course, as my mind's in a higher orbit,
But I'm blessed with such an aura or, should I say, a power,
That men, like honey bees, build their dreams around my flower.

CHRISTOPHER:
  Men? What men?
AMANDA:
             Oh, Lycidas, Joshua, Sebastian and Norbert.
VADIUS:
  What, all at once?
AMANDA:
             Ah, yes! They love me with all their might.
CHRISTOPHER:
  They have told you this?
AMANDA:
             No, they'd not dare express it as such,
  As, to this very day, they have respected me far too much,
  And none is sufficiently literate to get all the syntax right,
  So they offer me their hearts in a kind of silent coma,
  Which I find far more enchanting, having an element of grace.
CHRISTOPHER:
  Well, we hardly ever see Lycidas hanging about the place.
AMANDA:
  Yes, he's not so much a presence as a kind of distant aroma.
CHRISTOPHER:
  And Joshua says you're a monster!
AMANDA:
             Only out of jealous affection.
CHRISTOPHER:
  And Sebastian and Norbert?
VADIUS:
             I was speaking to a colleague's
    mother
  Who told me Sebastian and Norbert had recently married each
    other.
AMANDA:
  A somewhat desperate response to my cool and unwavering
    rejection.

ACT TWO

VADIUS:
> Goodness me, my dear Amanda, I'd say you're suffering from visions.

CHRISTOPHER:
> I think the word is *'chimeras'*—and you really should expel them.

AMANDA:
> Chimeras, *moi*? My poor lovers! I'll nimbly rush to tell them
> They're chimeras and whimsical whimeras, all of them mere apparitions!

SCENE FOUR

CHRISTOPHER, VADIUS.

CHRISTOPHER:
> My daughter's mad.

VADIUS:
> Yes. There's enough there for a convention.

CHRISTOPHER:
> It gets worse every day. Sorry about that little distraction.

VADIUS:
> As I was saying, Clinton has expressed his great attraction
> To Juliet, and to marry her is clearly his intention.
> What answer should I give him in response to his request?

CHRISTOPHER:
> Does he even need to ask? I consent with all my heart,
> In fact I would be honoured; I liked him right from the start.

VADIUS:
> You do know he has no money—

CHRISTOPHER:
> In that, I have no interest.
> He is rich in virtue, which to me is better than pure gold,
> And his father and I were inseparable, as alike as two peas.

VADIUS:
> Well, let's consult Philomena, to make sure that she agrees.

CHRISTOPHER:
> No need to. Just tell Clinton that I welcome him to the fold.

VADIUS:
> Yes, but for the sake of harmony, should we not have your wife's consent?

CHRISTOPHER:
> Don't be silly; as I said it's unnecessary what you propose,
> Because I speak for my wife, and so what I say goes.

VADIUS:
> But—

CHRISTOPHER:
>   Leave it to me; don't worry! She'll agree a hundred percent.
> When a daughter wishes to marry, her father receives a boost,
> Because it provides an opportunity to show who rules the roost;
> My authority in this family is as solid as a proverbial rock;
> The hen doesn't decide this matter; this is a job for the cock.

SCENE FIVE

PHILOMENA, CHRISTOPHER.

PHILOMENA:
> You!? Choose a husband!? Ha! Are there any more bombshells to drop?

CHRISTOPHER:
> No. And there's nothing to fight about. The subject's closed—
>
> *He goes to leave.*

PHILOMENA:
>   Stop!
> The subject is wide open, buster, like a half-gutted mackerel. So:
> Number one, it's Amanda's turn, as you should very well know;
> She is our elder daughter! And she should be first to marry;
> Number two, Juliet won't be wed to some Tom, Dick or Harry.

CHRISTOPHER:
> Number one, our elder daughter has a definite distaste for marriage.
> She's a perversely celibate philosopher whom I don't like to disparage,

ACT TWO

But, though we've raised her as best we can, and done a very
   good job,
Despite our sincere efforts, she's an astronomical snob.
And number two, our younger daughter has her heart firmly set
On a very particular husband—

PHILOMENA:
                       I have a husband for Juliet.

CHRISTOPHER:
What?

PHILOMENA:
   It's Tristan Tosser.

CHRISTOPHER:
                  Tristan Tosser? But the man's a fraud!

PHILOMENA:
The mere fact that this honourable man has failed to strike a chord
By clawing his way into your esteem, is of no consequence at all:
He is a writer.

CHRISTOPHER:
          A third-rate poet!

PHILOMENA:
                      Hush!

CHRISTOPHER:
                       Look, I don't want a brawl.

PHILOMENA:
There won't be a brawl, because there won't be further
   discussion.
My mind is made up!

CHRISTOPHER:
                 But you must be suffering from concussion!

PHILOMENA:
I am a far better judge than you of whether a man has worth;
If it were left to you, there'd be mismatches crashing all over the
   earth.
Now: it is quite superfluous to suffer your ludicrous views,
And don't say a word to Juliet; I want to give her the news.

So I will talk to her first, before you fill her head with pollution.
I'll make her listen to reason so she'll accept my resolution.
And if you interfere and warn her, I will easily be able to tell;
Your intercession in family affairs leaves a very noxious smell.

SCENE SIX

CHRISTOPHER, MARTINA.

MARTINA:
Jeez, just my rotten luck! It's always me that's to blame!
If ya want to hang a good dog, first ya give it a bad name.
It's a mug's game being a domestic; ya get bugger all out if it.

CHRISTOPHER:
What? Martina? What's the matter?

MARTINA:
                        Ya just get treated like shit.

CHRISTOPHER:
Eh?

MARTINA:
    I've been given me notice.

CHRISTOPHER:
                        Your notice!?

MARTINA:
                        Missus gave me the sack.

CHRISTOPHER:
What? I know nothing of this!

MARTINA:
                    She said get out and never come back.
She threatened me that if I didn't piss off, she'd kick the crap out of me.

CHRISTOPHER:
No, no, I'm not having any of that. You do your job perfectly.
Sometimes my wife can tend to be a little, you know, hot-headed.

MARTINA:
> Oh, man, she's gone, like, AWOL.

CHRISTOPHER:
> She can be bit flighty.

MARTINA:
> You said it.
> I wanted to give her this letter. It's, um, from some big-shot lawyer.
> I s'pose I can give it to you, since she's, like, no longer my employer.

SCENE SEVEN

PHILOMENA, MARTINA, CHRISTOPHER, AMANDA.

PHILOMENA:
> What? Do my eyes deceive me or are you still here, you guttersnipe?
> You're as common as muck! Get out! We just don't want your type!

CHRISTOPHER:
> She has a letter for you, and perhaps one you oughtn't—

PHILOMENA rips up the letter and throws it away.

> —Ignore…

PHILOMENA:
> [*To* MARTINA] Now get out and stay out!

CHRISTOPHER:
> [*Re the letter*] I hope that wasn't important.

PHILOMENA:
> And never come anywhere near me! Go on! Get out of my sight!

CHRISTOPHER:
> Now just calm down.

PHILOMENA:
> No, it's done!

CHRISTOPHER:
                            Look—
PHILOMENA:
                                    I want her gone, right?
CHRISTOPHER:
But what has she done wrong to merit being treated this way?
PHILOMENA:
What, you mean you support her?
CHRISTOPHER:
                                I merely ask why she can't stay?
PHILOMENA:
So you take her side against me?
CHRISTOPHER:
                            Heavens, no! But tell me her crime!
PHILOMENA:
Do you think I would dismiss her with no reason or rhyme?
CHRISTOPHER:
I didn't say that; but surely we must treat everyone the same.
We don't want to get ourselves caught up in some power game.
PHILOMENA:
No, she has to go, I said! I want her out of the place!
CHRISTOPHER:
Oh, well, yes, okay, if you think you have a strong case.
PHILOMENA:
I will in no way tolerate having my decisions contradicted.
CHRISTOPHER:
Alright!
PHILOMENA:
            As a reasonable husband, where two sides are conflicted,
You should ally yourself with me, and assume my rage as yours.
CHRISTOPHER:
And I do. Yes, my wife is right and she obviously has good cause
To run you out of the house, you miscreant; go on, get out of here.
MARTINA:
But what the hell have I done?

ACT TWO

CHRISTOPHER:
[*Aside to her*] I have absolutely no idea.
PHILOMENA:
As you can see, her attitude shows not the slightest remorse.
CHRISTOPHER:
We note your anger, dear heart, but are anxious to establish its source;
Has she broken a mirror, maybe, or some priceless porcelain, perhaps?
PHILOMENA:
Do you seriously imagine I'd send her packing for such a minor lapse?
If one wastes one's wrath on trivial matters, one has nothing in reserve.
CHRISTOPHER:
What can I say? So it's serious, then?
PHILOMENA:
Without doubt! What a nerve!
Do I strike you as an unreasonable woman, who goes off willy-nilly?
CHRISTOPHER:
Did her negligence leave us exposed to theft?
PHILOMENA:
Chris, don't be silly.
CHRISTOPHER:
So we didn't lose a precious vase or maybe a silver platter?
PHILOMENA:
It was nothing of the kind, and you well know that wouldn't matter.
CHRISTOPHER:
Oh my God! Don't tell me! She took money and failed to reimburse?
PHILOMENA:
It was far worse than that!
CHRISTOPHER:
Worse than that?

PHILOMENA:
> *Far* worse!

CHRISTOPHER:
Well, what the bloody hell did she do? Go to bed with the vicar?

PHILOMENA:
She has, with unequalled insolence, done something even sicker;
Despite some thirty lessons in how to speak correctly,
She has grossly insulted my ears by addressing me directly
With so brutal an abuse of words as to butcher our beautiful language;
Her ignorance of the Macquarie Dictionary causes terrible anguish.

CHRISTOPHER:
Oh, that.

PHILOMENA:
> Yes, that! And still, despite my robust remonstrations,

Explaining the science of language with specific demonstrations,
I am flummoxed and flabbergasted by the appalling things she'll say
As she trashes the laws of grammar, which even kings must obey.

CHRISTOPHER:
I thought she'd committed murder.

PHILOMENA:
> She has! To our native tongue!

What? You find it forgivable?

CHRISTOPHER:
> It's what she heard when she was young.

PHILOMENA:
I knew you'd try to excuse her!

CHRISTOPHER:
> Oh, I wouldn't dream of it.

PHILOMENA:
It really is pathetic—which is why I've made a theme of it—
That every grammatical construction she manages to destroy,
As if she deliberately chooses, with whatever means she can deploy,

ACT TWO

To tear down the rules of speech in which she's been carefully instructed.

MARTINA:
Um, yeah, like, whatever. Sorry. It seems like I totally fucked it.
I feel a bit, like, vunerable, when I get stuck in this kind of sitch.
I should of spoken better, but find proper talk a bit of a bitch,
I ain't got the balls for niceties, like I'm not one wiff mental strenth,
But to do a roolly good day's work, I'll go to pretty much any lenth.

PHILOMENA:
'Um, yeah, like, whatever.' Exactly which language is that in?
And 'vunerable' has an L, it's from *'vulnus'*, a wound, in Latin.
God knows what is meant by 'sitch', and you should *have* spoken better.
And '*StrenGth*' and '*LenGth*' have a G, the seventh alphabetical letter!

MARTINA:
Yeah, right, but what youse are spewin' is all very well and good,
But since talkin' like you doesn't get nowhere, not sure why I should.

PHILOMENA:
The impudent little wretch sees correctness as some odious duty,
Instead of using it as something founded on reason and poetic beauty.

MARTINA:
Don't think I'm not, like, grateful or nuthin' for the rooles you hand me,
But um the reason I don't change nuthin' is that people understand me.

PHILOMENA:
What style she has! 'I don't change nuthin''!

AMANDA:
                                 And it's a double negative too.
'Don't' with 'noth*ing*' is what we call redundant—just like you.

MARTINA:
Oh my God! Like, give me a break; I'm not a scholar, okay!
People who are brung up like me always talk this way.

PHILOMENA:
The woman's a walking earache;
AMANDA:
                        Such solecism!
PHILOMENA:
                                 Expression is dead!
AMANDA:
I wish you were all subtext, Martina, leaving *everything* unsaid. You haven't a clue about singular or plural, or any sense of grammar.
MARTINA:
That ain't true! I always look after my grandpa and gramma!
PHILOMENA:
God Almighty.
MARTINA:
                Me and Gramma—
PHILOMENA:
                        'Grandma and I—'
MARTINA:
                                   —Are mates, but.
PHILOMENA:
She begins with 'me' and ends with 'but'!
MARTINA:
                              Yeah, but—
PHILOMENA:
                                 Keep your mouth shut.
AMANDA:
The woman is so appalling, she confuses the very word '*grammar*'! Every time she opens her mouth, it's like some relentless hammer.
PHILOMENA:
I have told you a hundred times where that word comes from!
MARTINA:
Like I care if it comes from Mars or the backside of Christendom.

ACT TWO

AMANDA:
What a peasant! Grammar teaches you to tell a verb from a noun,
The nominative, the subjunctive—
MARTINA:
                                Who are they? Are they new in town?
PHILOMENA:
Oh, agony!
AMANDA:
                They are parts of speech and all of them have to agree.
MARTINA:
Who gives a stuff if they don't get on? Not everyone agrees with me.
PHILOMENA:
[*To* AMANDA] Put an end to this hideous discussion!
[*To* CHRISTOPHER]   And for Godsake send her away!
CHRISTOPHER:
As you wish. Martina, my dear, I am really sorry to say
That we'd better not upset her further; be a dear lady and off you pop.
PHILOMENA:
Why do you speak to her gently? You sound like an absolute sop!
You treat her like marshmallow, when what she deserves is a wallop!
You are such a wuss! Are you afraid you might offend this trollop?
CHRISTOPHER:
Not at all; she is in no doubt about your decision to shaft her;
[*Loudly*] Go on, off you go! [*Gently*] Don't worry, I'll see you're looked after.

SCENE EIGHT

PHILOMENA, CHRISTOPHER, AMANDA.

CHRISTOPHER:
Well, there you are, she's gone; so I hope you're satisfied,

But I don't approve at all of how the poor woman was tried
Like a criminal; she was good at the things for which we hired her;
And now, for some trivial transgression, you've gone and fired her.

PHILOMENA:
Do you expect me to retain that woman in my service, forever
Subjecting my poor ears to cruel torture whenever
She speaks, flouting every law of oral communication
With such barbaric dollops of gross bastardisation
And mutilated phrases that only a cretin would utter,
Strung together with gunge, like something dragged from the gutter?

CHRISTOPHER:
Sorry, I've forgotten the question.

AMANDA:
Look, she was truly appalling,
And ripping the dictionary to pieces is very deeply galling.
Even her smallest offences, like repetition and tautology,
Are the most egregious insult to one versed in philology.

CHRISTOPHER:
So she doesn't know the dictionary; she's not a bloody linguist;
Does it matter? It's the kitchen where her talents are distinguished.
I have to say I'd much prefer that she choose the right herbs,
Even if, while doing so, she mightn't use the right verbs;
I'd rather she repeat a hundred times some inappropriate phrase
Than burn the roast, congeal the soup or screw the *bouillabaisse*.
When I'm having a bowl of soup, accompanied by a little tipple
I'm not there thinking how I'd kill for a perfect participle.
I mean, Molière and Shakespeare, sure, they put language on the map,
But stick them in a kitchen, and they might be absolute crap.

PHILOMENA:
This is an outrage. From the moment your tirade began,
I was discombobulated by the effrontery that you call yourself a man,
Yet you lower yourself unceasingly to the pits of material filth
Rather than raise your sights towards your intellectual health.

You dare to mention your stomach, and worse, you would even stoop
To compare Molière with mutton, and Shakespeare with soup!
Our body is but a mortal rag, which our soul leaves far behind.

CHRISTOPHER:
But as this rag is actually me, the rag must be wined and dined.

AMANDA:
The body and the mind, dear father, are united in one being,
But if you accept what learnèd people have no difficulty seeing,
Then the mind, rather than the body, has clear superiority
And to nourish it with the sap of science is our first priority.

CHRISTOPHER:
Bollocks. Whatever you're feeding your mind, I'm in no rush to try it,
As it seems to me your mental menu is a sadly inadequate diet.
You don't care how badly you treat people, if you're unfair or rude,
Because you haven't the faintest interest in human solicitude.
[*Re Martina*] That poor woman—

PHILOMENA:
                          Oh, *solicitude*! No-one uses that word anymore;
It reeks of straight-laced and old-fashioned;

AMANDA:
                                  I've never heard it before.

CHRISTOPHER:
You want to know what I think? I'm sorry, but I have to come clean!
So it's off with this mask of civility; I'm going to vent my spleen:
[*To* AMANDA] People out there think you're mad! And in my heart I can only agree.

AMANDA:
Oh, here we go. What now?

CHRISTOPHER:
                       Just shut up and listen to me!
The slightest error in words will send you into a spin,
But you'll tolerate far worse in actions, without the least chagrin.

That pile of luminous poetry and that mountain of books you've got
Have taught you no humanity, so you might as well burn the lot!
What's the point of a titanic dictionary, pronouncing on all things oral,
If you get to page one thousand and forty, with no idea of what's moral?
And all those volumes on science! I mean, do you really need them?
The difference between you and scientists is that they actually read them.
You said you read a history by Plutarch, for something to do in bad weather,
Yet when I used it to press my ties, its pages were still joined together.
And I wish you'd remove that telescope, which is especially problematic,
As it frightens the hell out of the neighbours, and takes up most of the attic.
When your own patch of earth is in tatters, what the hell is the purpose
Of ignoring it completely while you examine the lunar surface?
Everything in your personal life is completely upside down,
While you parade this bookish pomposity all over the bloody town.

AMANDA:
So you'd prefer me surrounded by children, out at the clothesline, pegging—

CHRISTOPHER:
No, but to consume yourself so that everything else goes begging—

AMANDA:
You sound just like men of yesterday, your forefathers and such,
Who thought if a woman knew anything, she already knew too much.
Confine her to domestic economy, keeping house, training underlings;

ACT TWO

    The only philosophy called for was a needle and thread and such
        things;
    Her idea of science was to tell a shirt from a pair of pants;
    And she was raised to see her wedding day as the pinnacle of
        romance.
    The house was to be her universe and her only learnèd conversation
    Was about the deadly tedious ritual of wifely domestication.

CHRISTOPHER:
    That is not the point! And nor is it my point of view;
    Knowledge is an aspiration that every one ought to pursue,
    Not telling your sister that getting married is some kind of deadly
        curse,
    While you pretend to be mistress of every subject in the universe;
    If you really knew anything, you'd be at the university teaching it,
    Instead of prancing all over the place and so piously preaching it.

AMANDA:
    But I've heard you say there are too many women deciding to be
        writers;

CHRISTOPHER:
    What I said was, women *or* men, there are too many of the
        blighters!
    They seem to pop up everywhere, as if we somehow breed them;
    With so many people writing, it's a wonder there's anyone to read
        them.
    And there are people who *cannot* write, re-writing writers who
        could,
    And giving us appalling versions of works that used to be good.
    And there are some ingenious non-writers, of whom I'm sure
        you've heard,
    Who can adapt a foreign writer, in whose language they don't
        know a word.

PHILOMENA:
    They don't all have to *be* writers, but I insist they know *how* to
        write;
    Which is why I only want staff who are equipped with reason and
        light.

CHRISTOPHER:
> 'Reason', my dear Philly, seems to have taken over the entire house:
> Most people have a rat in their pantry; we have an over-educated mouse.
> I really have no idea what this obsession with reason is about,
> Given that all this reasoning has driven reason out!

PHILOMENA:
> The staff like to be learnèd, as they know it pleases me.

CHRISTOPHER:
> I asked for a drink yesterday; it was delivered with poetry.

PHILOMENA:
> You have an attitude to learnèd people, which underscores all you say.

CHRISTOPHER:
> I have an attitude to *pretension* as I suffer it night and day!
> Knowledge is a gift, not a weapon or a key to some ivory tower;
> One should share it like wisdom, not strut it like arrogant power;
> One should use knowledge for employment; or enjoy it for its own sake;
> When knowledge is used for snobbery, then knowledge, my dears, is fake!
> One should bear it with humility, not wear it like a crown!
> *You* don't use knowledge to build people up, *you* use it to put people down!
> Like Martina, a kitchen maid, who—

PHILOMENA:
>   *Whom*—

CHRISTOPHER:
>   —You've chucked out on the street
> Because in your kingdom of language, the poor woman can't compete!
> So she's a little bit illiterate; every creature has its louse,
> But in her own way Martina brought some wisdom to the house.

PHILOMENA:
> All my attempts to guide you on the riddling road to illumination

ACT TWO

Have obviously failed completely to elicit appreciation.

CHRISTOPHER:
Oh I see, I merely have opinions, whereas you *appreciate*?
Then how come you welcome such charlatans into our house of late?

AMANDA:
Charlatans? What charlatans?

CHRISTOPHER:
Tristan Tosser, just for starters.

PHILOMENA:
You envy his style.

CHRISTOPHER:
Rubbish! I'd have his guts for garters.
You've been eardrummed and brainwashed by his unutterable twaddle
And just because he knows Latin, you hold him up as some model.
After he speaks, one has no idea exactly what he just said,
And yet you'd inflict him on our daughter, insisting they be wed.
Don't think they'd ever be happy like some Joan and Darby,
Because trust me: the man's one sausage sanger short of a barbie.

PHILOMENA:
How gross, oh God, how tasteless, both in language and in soul!

AMANDA:
How such vulgar little atoms could make up a composite whole!
And how could a mind formed of such common corpuscles
Share the same blood as me, the same genes, limbs and muscles?
I would much rather be dead than be a member of your race!
I will depart from you at once in a desperate attempt to save face.

PHILOMENA:
And Juliet will become Madame Tosser if it's the last thing I do.
And on this subject I must insist I hear nothing more from you!

SCENE NINE

VADIUS, CHRISTOPHER.

VADIUS:
Well, how did it go? I saw Philomena leaving as I came in.

So, was it a success? Does Clinton have Juliet?
I take it your wife consented? So, then, we're all set?
I mean, you did have a little chat?

CHRISTOPHER:
                                      Where shall I begin?

VADIUS:
  She agreed?

CHRISTOPHER:
               Not quite; not yet;

VADIUS:
                         She refused?

CHRISTOPHER:
                                Refused? No, no.

VADIUS:
  So, she's undecided then?

CHRISTOPHER:
                        My wife?! You'll pardon my guffaw.
In fact she suggested someone else to be our son-in-law.

VADIUS:
  Someone else?

CHRISTOPHER:
               Yes, someone else.

VADIUS:
                           Oh. Anyone I know?

CHRISTOPHER:
  Oh, yes.

VADIUS:
     What's his name?

CHRISTOPHER:
                   Tristan Tosser.

VADIUS:
                           What!? You don't mean—

CHRISTOPHER:
  Yes.

ACT TWO

VADIUS:
    You didn't accept, I hope!
CHRISTOPHER:
        Dear God, certainly not.
VADIUS:
    So what did you say?
CHRISTOPHER:
        Well, nothing much—She had me on the spot;
    Other than to say his Latin verses were a kind of verbal latrine,
    At the mention of his name, I thought I should stay uncommitted.
VADIUS:
    But did you at least inform her Clinton was a suitable alternative?
CHRISTOPHER:
    I was so shocked, my dear Athénaïs, I erred on the side of
        conservative.
VADIUS:
    Ah yes, I'm sure your reason's sound, and your prudence well-
        acquitted,
    But—
CHRISTOPHER:
        It somehow seemed unhelpful to throw another hat in the ring.
VADIUS:
    But did you not feel some regret at your display of meekness?
    I worry that your dear wife may perceive that as a weakness.
    Your restraint on this point is surely a remarkable thing,
    As neither party to a marriage should make the decisions alone.
CHRISTOPHER:
    My God! My dear Athénaïs, that's so easy for you to say;
    You and your husband *share* decisions!
VADIUS:
        We would have it no other
    way.
    Neither one should bully the other by taking a superior tone.
CHRISTOPHER:
    You've no idea of how her savage tongue weighs down upon me;

If darling Philly does her block you can hear it a mile away;
When she gets on her high horse, by God, she can give you a spray.
I much prefer tranquillity, peace and quiet, domestic harmony.
If I raise the slightest opposition, I just end up being fearful—

VADIUS:
But you'd think her lofty morality and contempt for property and money
Would calm her turbulent temper, like a kind of intellectual honey.

CHRISTOPHER:
On the contrary, I endure a week of hell, and cop one almighty earful.
I'm absolutely terrified if she's alone with me;
You have to realise what it's like being daily accosted;
If I'd pushed her about Clinton, she would have completely lost it.
She's a dragon full of fire, and when she takes that tone with me,
I call her Dear Heart and Sweetie-Pie.

VADIUS:
                                        Then the fault lies with you, too:
You can't blame Philomena for being strong, and making a firm decision:
It's your weakness that gives her strength, your timidity augments her position.
It's not your wife, but your own cowardice, that reigns supreme over you.
Marriage is an institution, which has rules, like any polity.
If you stoop, you lend her height; if you cringe, you increase her authority;
Hand her the halter, you'll be led by the nose, as you place her in seniority.
Marriage can't function in harmony if you abandon the concept of equality.

CHRISTOPHER:
Equality? She fired the kitchen maid; guess who'll be doing the dishes?

VADIUS:
>   Can someone as precious as your daughter be devalued or underpriced?
>   How will you live without shame, if Juliet is sacrificed?

CHRISTOPHER:
>   Do you really believe that Philomena would condescend to my wishes?

VADIUS:
>   May I share with you something that bears on your present state?
>   In Africa, there's a part of a jungle, where the underbrush is so dense
>   That the butterflies find it impossible to see each other, and hence
>   They fly high above a mountain, and there they find a mate.
>   My parents wanted me to marry a brilliant biologist.
>   Instead, I chose a simple man, which they thought was not a good start;
>   That is, until they had a glimpse of the goodness in his heart.
>   So they gave us their blessing as it was what we dearly wished.
>   If we make the ground rules so harsh that lovers can't see each other,
>   Like some oppressive jungle, where the light can't penetrate,
>   Then they'll fly above that mountain where they will choose their mate.
>   We lose them both forever, but they will have one another.
>   Your family is currently possessed by a most ridiculous delusion:
>   A man with six words of Latin has bound them in a spell,
>   And trying to get them to see the truth is a very hard sell.
>   To them, he's a writer of genius, who, in their state of confusion—
>   Though we know he makes a racing guide look like superior art—
>   They hail as a nouveau Socrates or Shakespeare, and there's the rub:
>   Not only is your entire house being turned into a book club
>   But this fraud might marry your daughter, and, in doing so, break her heart.
>   Come on! Once more I say, don't be a laughing stock;
>   Cowardice has no place, when your daughter's life is at stake.

CHRISTOPHER:
Yes, of course, you're right! Tristan Tosser's an absolute fake;
I must embolden my heart, and my courage I must unlock.
Thank you, dear friend, profoundly, for teaching me that I was wrong,

VADIUS:
Glad to be of help. And remember, I'm also a wife and mother.

CHRISTOPHER:
Yes, and now I see clearly: no spouse should smother the other.

VADIUS:
Anything you've heard from me was in your heart all along.

CHRISTOPHER:
I've been far too wishy-washy.

VADIUS:
                        True.

CHRISTOPHER:
                        And too submissive.

VADIUS:
                        Rather.

CHRISTOPHER:
Starting today I have to change, and make Philomena understand
If we're to be equal partners, then I play an equal part, *and*
That Juliet's my daughter too, and it follows that I'm her father.

VADIUS:
Unimpeachable logic.

CHRISTOPHER:
                        And I'll convince her of Juliet's choice
That Clinton is right for our daughter, whereas Tristan is a dunce.
You know where Clinton lives; tell him to come and see me at once.
The great thing with growing some balls, is it gives you a bit of a voice!

END OF ACT TWO

ACT THREE

SCENE ONE

PHILOMENA, AMANDA, TRISTAN TOSSER.

PHILOMENA:
> Welcome to the Tuesday Book Club! And hail to our Author of the Week!
> It's Tristan Tosser! and his stunning new work on which he's going to speak!

AMANDA:
> I burn to read it!

PHILOMENA:
> We're all on fire, just *dying* to inhale its pages!
> What oozes from your pen enthrals us, oh most lucid of sages!

AMANDA:
> Your unequalled eloquence caresses me with oils, which it's so rich in!

PHILOMENA:
> Yes, like a lingual banquet from some gorgeous gourmet kitchen!
> Please, let us suffer no longer in awaiting your aural perfection!

AMANDA:
> Do hasten!

PHILOMENA:
> Yes, quick! Thrust some gems in my general direction!

AMANDA:
> Soothe our impatient hunger with an epigrammatic orgasm!

PHILOMENA:
> Let your sumptuous syntax plunge deep through my ectoplasm!

TRISTAN:
> Ah, ladies, this book's like an infant, newborn unto the light.

AMANDA:
> God, don't you just *love* 'unto'!

TRISTAN:
                                      You've good reason to experience delight,
As it was in your very courtyard, with my mind electric and quivery,
That from the womb of my imagination, I finally effected delivery.

PHILOMENA:
The baby is more glorious, when one has the pleasure to know the father.

TRISTAN:
And may your radiant approbation serve as its surrogate mother.

AMANDA:
Pure genius!

SCENE TWO

PHILOMENA, AMANDA, TRISTAN, JULIET, CLINTON.

JULIET *enters, and turns immediately to leave.*

PHILOMENA:
                        Hang on, Juliet! Just where do you think you're going?

JULIET:
I mustn't disrupt your meeting; sorry, I entered without knowing—

PHILOMENA:
Don't go! Come and join us! We'll make up a fabulous foursome!
Treat your neglected ears to some intoxicating marvels!

JULIET:
                                                    Awesome;
But I don't really know very much about the nitty-gritty of writing;
It's not really my thing, so you wouldn't find me all that exciting.

PHILOMENA:
Don't be silly; and anyway, after this meeting is through
I have a lovely little secret, which I have to impart to you.

TRISTAN:
The literary arts are not something one should be frightened of,
Especially when you have other means of inspiring intimate love.

ACT THREE

JULIET:
Well, I'm not much good at either, actually—
TRISTAN:
Please, I implore you.
AMANDA:
Yes, open your mind to this newborn work of genius before you!

CLINTON *enters.* JULIET *is delighted.*

JULIET:
[*To him*] I didn't know you were here, Clint!
CLINTON:
[*To her*] Your father sent for me, Jules.
PHILOMENA:
Clinton! Make yourself useful! Fetch some chairs or comfortable stools.

CLINTON *does so, and on bringing chairs, has a spectacular fall.* JULIET *goes to him.*

You clumsy oaf! Haven't you learnt the principles of balance?
CLINTON:
I'm sorry, Madam, they fall outside the limits of my talents.
AMANDA:
Your fall, you ignorant man, is due to your mental depravity,
You strayed from a clear fixed point, which we call the centre of gravity.
CLINTON:
I am well aware of gravity, having fallen flat on my arse.
PHILOMENA:
How parlously prosaic!
TRISTAN:
It's a good thing he's not made of glass.
AMANDA:
What a brilliant riposte! Such dazzling wit, from poetry's high priest!

JULIET:
    [*Aside*] Are you okay, Clint?
CLINTON:
    [*With a smile*]   I'm fine, Jules.
PHILOMENA:
    [*To* TRISTAN]   Let us savour your feast.
TRISTAN:
    Video fames magna coram…
AMANDA:
                          I melt when he speaks in Latin!
CLINTON:
    [*To* JULIET] How strange, as Doctor Vadius says, it's a language he's a total pratt in.
TRISTAN:
    I see before me a great hunger, and for that reason, I suggest
    Instead of a mere eight lines, which would be a light *hors d'oeuvre* at best,
    I'd be doing well if I add to the epigram, or '*madrigal*', to be precise,
    A simmering taste of *ragout,* glazed with just a hint of spice:
    It makes a rather delectable entrée of a sonnet, addressed to a princess,
    And which I'm pleased to say, to her heart found felicitous ingress;
    And you will experience, I truly believe, a most exquisite delicacy;
    It is seasoned with the salt of Attica, infusèd by the Aegean Sea,
    Where my most elegiac Muse oft lowered her poetical anchor;
    I trust you may find it Elysian.
CLINTON:
    [*To* JULIET]   Oh God, what a wanker.
AMANDA:
    Who, with taste, could resist it?

    Each time TRISTAN *goes to read it,* AMANDA *interrupts.*

                          My heart vibrates with anticipation!

    TRISTAN *goes to read.*

ACT THREE

I love poetry with what you might call a doggèd captivation.

TRISTAN *goes to read.*

Especially when its verses are spun with such congruity.

PHILOMENA:
But if we don't stop talking, my dear, we won't hear any poetry.

TRISTAN:
'Sonn—'

AMANDA:
Juliet, hush!

TRISTAN:
'SONNET TO THE PRINCESS URANIE
ON THE SUBJECT OF HER FEVER'.
Your prudence must have gone to sleep
For you behaved so generously
And in your house so graciously
Your cruellest enemy did keep.

AMANDA:
Ah, what a pretty start! Each turn of phrase is so gallant!

PHILOMENA:
To him alone do verses flow in such abundant talent!

AMANDA:
'Prudence must have gone to sleep' disarmed all my defences.
And *'Your cruellest enemy did keep'* has bombarded my senses.

PHILOMENA:
'Generously' and *'graciously'* are so admirably adverbial.

AMANDA:
Let us brace our ears, for the pithy and proverbial.

TRISTAN:
Drive him out, whatever they say,
From your lavish residence;
This ingrate who would, without hesitance
Take your very life away.

AMANDA:
Stop! I am breathless! I need a moment to respire!

PHILOMENA:
>   Allow us, if you will, a little pause to admire.
>   One can actually feel these verses flow to the depth of the soul,
>   And a certain *je ne sais quoi* makes one swoon beyond control.

AMANDA:
>   '*Drive him out, whatever they say/From your lavish residence—*'
>   It's so—*pretty*! And so—*witty*! A metaphor of such eloquence!

PHILOMENA:
>   It's the '*Drive him out*', to my mind, that is pregnant with good taste,
>   A priceless expression, and so scrumptiously well-placed!

AMANDA:
>   But when coupled with '*whatever they say*', it causes my heart to twitch.

PHILOMENA:
>   I agree: '*whatever they say*' is like scratching a metaphorical itch.

AMANDA:
>   How I wish I'd written that! It's worth an entire collection!

PHILOMENA:
>   But do you ingest, as I do, all the flavours of this confection?

AMANDA:
>   Oh! Oh? [*After consideration*] Ohhhhh!

PHILOMENA:
>   'Drive him out!' 'Drive him out!'
>   As so often with a masterpiece, it's the subtext that inspires doubt.

AMANDA:
>   Ah! Yes!

PHILOMENA:
>   On one reading, the poet's mind is drawn to the fever;
>   But '*whatever they say*' refers to gossips who doubt the fever might leave her.
>   I personally would love to know if everyone here is the same as I,
>   In discovering for each phrase that a thousand interpretations apply?

ACT THREE 45

AMANDA:
>It's true that it says more things than the phrase itself imparts,
>For the whole is often greater than the sum of all its parts.

PHILOMENA:
>[*To* TRISTAN] But when you wrote this charming phrase,
>   '*whatever they say*',
>Did you yourself foresee the dazzling power it might convey?
>I mean, was it effortless and instinctive, or was it deliberate, I
>   wonder,
>To plant those hidden layers for us to plumb and plunder?

TRISTAN:
>[*Mysteriously*] Ahhh! Wellll—

AMANDA:
>   And how '*ingrate*' has lodged in my
>   head!
>This *ingrate* of a fever, so iniquitous and ill-bred,
>Which *ingratiates* itself so treacherously in those it occupies.

PHILOMENA:
>So far both the quatrains have been a most arresting surprise;
>Let us come now to the triplets, which will be equally sublime.

>   TRISTAN *goes to read.*

AMANDA:
>Ah, but do you mind if I hear *ingrate* just one more time?

TRISTAN:
>*Drive him out, whatever they say—*

AMANDA:
>   —How easily it falls from the lip.

TRISTAN:
>*From your lavish residence—*

AMANDA:
>   —Here it comes, now let it rip!

TRISTAN:
>*This ingrate—*

AMANDA:
>   —Oh Goddd!

TRISTAN:
>   *Who would—*

AMANDA:
>   It's the thinking girl's
chocolate éclaire!
And as for '*lavish residence*', I think I'm going to slide off the chair.

TRISTAN:
Take your very life away.

PHILOMENA:
>   It's the '*very*' that's the icing on top!

AMANDA:
I can't imagine anything better than '*away*' to precede a full stop.

TRISTAN:
> *What? Without respect for your rank,*
> *From your blood this monster drank;*

AMANDA & PHILOMENA:
Ah!

TRISTAN:
> *The outrage persists night and day!*
> *If you go to your bath, take him down,*
> *Then bargain no longer, I pray,*
> *And by your own hands let him drown.*

PHILOMENA:
I'm quite overwhelmed!

AMANDA:
>   I faint! One could actually die of such
treasures!

PHILOMENA:
Now I know how it feels to be seized by a thousand pleasures!

AMANDA:
'*If you go to your bath, take him down—*'

PHILOMENA:
>   '*And by your own hands let*
him drown.'

ACT THREE

    By your very own hands ... drown him ... right there ... in the bath water!
AMANDA:
    Every moment of the verse builds up to this charming slaughter.
PHILOMENA:
    One promenades through these verses in a kind of ravenous stupor;
AMANDA:
    And the things upon which one treads are all transcendentally super;
PHILOMENA:
    As if we have entered a realm where everything is sacred and holy,
    Like passing through little paths, all strewn with gladioli.
TRISTAN:
    So you like the poem, then?
PHILOMENA:
                            It's a riveting and marvellous sonnet;
    No-one's done anything better.
AMANDA:
                            So Jules, what are your thoughts on it?
    Or are these succulent morsels too refined for your untutored gullet?
PHILOMENA:
    Right through this entire reading, you've sat there like a stunned mullet.
JULIET:
    Each of us here below plays a part as best we can,
    A great mind is not something I just decide to be better than.
TRISTAN:
    Perhaps my verses disturb you?
JULIET:
                            I don't know, because I wasn't
        listening.

PHILOMENA:
Let's move on to the birth of the epigram!
AMANDA:
                                    Like witnesses at a christening!
TRISTAN:
        'CONCERNING A CARRIAGE OF REDDISH-ROSE,
              BEING A GIFT TO A LADY FRIEND'
PHILOMENA:
Catchy title!
AMANDA:
                It really grabs you.
PHILOMENA:
                             It's so unexpected, so rare.
AMANDA:
It opens the door to a hundred joys and the road that will take you there.
TRISTAN:
                      Love—

AMANDA & PHILOMENA:
Ah!
TRISTAN:
> *Love sells its bonds for a princely sum*
> *And a less wealthy man have I now become*
> *For behold this coach most beautiful and bold*
> *With its bas-relief of such perfect gold*
> *That it stuns all the lands it passes by*
> *Raising the glory of my Laïs on high—*
> *Say no more—*

PHILOMENA:
Ah, '*my Laïs*'! How Greek! Now there is true erudition.
TRISTAN:
                   Say no more—
AMANDA:
The words themselves are gold! What a lustrous composition.

ACT THREE

TRISTAN:
>*Say no more of its rose-red hue*
>*But that it pays my debt to you.*

AMANDA:
Who would have seen that coming?

PHILOMENA:
>What good taste to leave the best till last.

Let's hear it for our Writer of the Week! You've left us all quite aghast!

Applause.

I don't know, from the moment we met, if I was predisposed in your favour,
But I admire your verse and your prose as something precious to savour.

TRISTAN:
Madam is most gratifying; might it be appropriate to enquire
If perhaps you have something yourself that I might, in turn, admire?

PHILOMENA:
I have written nothing in verse, but I have good reason to expect
That I will soon be able to show you, out of friendship and respect,
Eight chapters outlining my plan for a women's academy;
I am taking Plato's skeletal framework and giving it anatomy.
And the most exciting project on which the Academy will be employed
Is a very noble enterprise, at which I am overjoyed;
A glorious undertaking, which will be lavishly lauded
When the history of great minds is ultimately recorded;
We will achieve what many claim to be humanly unfulfillable:
The removal from our language of every unpleasant syllable,
Those sounds which crudely accompany an otherwise beautiful word
And which are so insulting to our ear, that they'd be better left unheard,

> For though they amuse the groundlings, they make the judicious
>   grieve
> With dirty double meanings, which naughty boys thrill to conceive,
> In those sickening public places, where the illiterati congregate
> To insult our human decency through the language they mutilate.

TRISTAN:
> What an ardent cause and a dithyrambic articulation!

PHILOMENA:
> You will see all our laws when they are ready for publication.

AMANDA:
> We will be, by those laws, the judges of all expression
> And all prose and all verse will be subject to our discretion.
> Only we and our friends will decide what passes for wit,
> And those outside the club will be regarded as counterfeit.
> No-one will become a member except at our inviting
> And we alone will rule on what amounts to good writing.

JULIET and CLINTON *try to leave.*

PHILOMENA:
> Wait! Juliet! I thought I made it perfectly clear
> I have something to say to you, so I need you to stay here.

JULIET:
> But I have no business here;

PHILOMENA:
> Yes, you do, as you'll soon see.

JULIET:
> Well, for the life of me, I can't imagine what it could be.

TRISTAN:
> I am curious to hear a word from the young man who brought
>   chairs;
> He makes no contribution; he simply sits and stares.
> What think you, dare I ask, of Aristotle's peripatetic school?

CLINTON:
> I have no considered opinion;

AMANDA:
> On Aristotle, Clinton's a fool.

ACT THREE 51

TRISTAN:
On the magnetism of Descartes?
AMANDA:
Clinton finds it hard to endure us.
TRISTAN:
Perhaps you lean to Lucretius? Or have a penchant for Epicurus?
Lucretius demystified the gods in his incandescent *De Rerum Natura*—
CLINTON:
Well, I look forward to having a squiz, maybe when I'm a bit maturer.
TRISTAN:
Mmm. What think you, then, of the realm of Platonic abstraction?
CLINTON:
Not a lot;
AMANDA:
It's hardly a field, which for Clinton, holds much attraction,
Is it, darling?
CLINTON:
Well—
JULIET:
Amanda!
AMANDA:
In his *Republic*, Plato asks
Why women should not share equally in all of men's tasks;
And he struck another blow for women, in an argument well-polished
That the traditional nuclear family really should be abolished.
You claim, my dear Jules, that my position is demonic,
But it turns out, in fact, that I am simply neo-Platonic.
PHILOMENA:
When he drafted his *Republic*, the subject of women arose,
And I've come to see it as some kind of personal challenge, I suppose,
To avenge the female sex of all the wrongs done to us

By writing one all-embracing and voluminous omnibus,
Illustrating the indignity of placing limits on the female mind
By subjecting us to trivial tasks, to which our talents were confined,
And closing the door to knowledge and hiding from our sight
The grandeur of the universe and its sublime interior light.

TRISTAN:
Brava! My position on women is well known and it won't surprise;
That if I render homage to the splendour of your eyes
I also raise your minds in Platonic exaltation
And humbly take my place in your literary emancipation.

SCENE THREE

TRISTAN, PHILOMENA, AMANDA, JULIET, CLINTON, VADIUS.

DOCTOR VADIUS *enters. She has heard the last exchange.*

VADIUS:
I'm afraid you are mistaken; from Plato we have much to learn,
But he was not bothered about women's *rights*, only with their
    usefulness.
Yes, women could do what men do, but in all truthfulness,
This was a community benefit, a purely practical concern.
He was hardly a trumpeting herald for women's liberation
Just because he thought domesticity a waste of woman-power;
Working in an office or factory would hardly rupture her flower;
If she were strong enough, why should there be any differentiation?
And as for the nuclear family, he saw it a waste of talents
To have a good teacher stuck at home acting as a nursery maid;
If she has administrative skills or a leaning towards a trade
Then spending all day on children was unproductive, on balance.
And having female nannies to take care of someone else's offspring
Relegated these females to a kind of inferior status.
You could just as well have *au pair* boys to fill that hiatus;
So the grand communal nursery, to Plato, was just a practical thing.

TRISTAN:
Doctor Athénaïs Vadius, what a pleasure to hear erudition!
Of the Greek and Latin authors, you have such eloquent
    command;

ACT THREE

If I partook of the error, then I accept your reprimand.
And I assure you, of this mistake, there will be no repetition.

PHILOMENA:
Learnèd Doctor Vadius, your reputation is beyond doubt.
And, God, can one restrain oneself on anything Latin or Greek?

AMANDA:
I have just become moist! Did someone Greek speak?

JULIET:
You'll excuse me, I don't know Greek, so I had better bow out.

VADIUS:
Must you go?

PHILOMENA:
[*Stopping her*] Juliet!

VADIUS:
[*To* JULIET] I was rather eager to see you;
[*To them*] Those welcoming words bid me to stay, if I'm not disturbing,
And provided my presence in this hallowed circle is not perturbing—

PHILOMENA:
Au contraire! Every woman secretly wants to be you!
And one learnèd in Greek at any gathering, is an improvement.

TRISTAN:
As Doctor Vadius is a leading light on both verse and prose,
She might herself have something to read us, if we may so propose?

VADIUS:
You're too kind, but I must be honest: In the literary movement,
I see it as a fault in authors, with the works that they write,
To dominate the company and every conversation,
And whether it be at cafés, dinner tables or some celebration,
To bore the guests to death with a book from which they recite.
To me, there's nothing more pathetic, no practice I more abhor,
Than writers going about, almost begging for praise,
And earbashing the first people who happen to meet their gaze,
Who very often are the martyrs whom they bored the night before.
I am opposed to this self-promotion; on this I remain avowed,

And I remember a certain Greek—
AMANDA & PHILOMENA:
         Ah!
VADIUS:
           —Under whose influence I fell,
Who proposed a specific law, whereby he would expel
Any writers who felt the urge to read their own works aloud.
It is for others, not myself, to read any works of mine.
[*Giving them:*] If you wish, take this ballad; it's dedicated to young lovers;
TRISTAN:
[*Perusing it*] These verses have a lyrical beauty quite unavailable to others.
Venus and all the Graces reign, and in your poems they shine.
You have a flowing turn of phrase, each word the perfect choice.
It is suffusèd with ethos, and pathos is ubiquitous,
Like the 'Eclogues of Virgil' and the 'Idylls of Theocritus';
Your odes have a noble air, and they sing with a gallant voice,
So sweetly rendered, that they make dear Horace seem second-rate.
Is there anything so romantic as your lovely *chansonettes*?
Your sonnets are bejewelled with gems one never forgets.
The rondos and the madrigals are so adorably ornate;
If this country did you justice, if you were recognised by this age,
You would sit atop a gilded carriage, being borne from place to place,
Your statues would adorn our streets, and stamps would bear your face,
For the genius of your *oeuvre* explodes on every page.
VADIUS:
I am a humble servant of language;
CLINTON:
         No, you're a true high achiever!
VADIUS:
Clinton, you are passionate, and I place great value on it.

ACT THREE

TRISTAN:
> Have you, by any chance, heard of a certain recent sonnet,
> 'To the Princess Uranie, On the Subject of Her Fever'?

VADIUS:
> Yes, as a matter of fact, it was read to me yesterday.

TRISTAN:
> Do you know who the author is?

VADIUS:
>   I haven't the faintest clue,
> But one thing I do know is: it's not worth a brass razoo.

TRISTAN:
> A great many people, in fact, find it admirable, so they say.

VADIUS:
> That doesn't prevent it from being awful, or being laughed at,
> And if you had also read it, you would share my point of view.

TRISTAN:
> I fear that on this matter, I simply cannot agree with you.
> Very few writers, if any, could write such a sonnet as that.

VADIUS:
> True; it would take an alarming absence of taste and poetic flair
> To think up such drivel in the first place, and then actually write it
>   down.

TRISTAN:
> I cannot concur; it could only be written by a poet of great renown.

VADIUS:
> God preserve us! If I'd written that, I'd shoot myself then and there.

TRISTAN:
> I have a very sound reason for liking it.

VADIUS:
>   Oh?

TRISTAN:
>   The sonnet was written
>   by me.

VADIUS:
> You!

TRISTAN:
> Yes, me.

VADIUS:
> I'm so sorry. How on earth could I have missed the point?

TRISTAN:
> It is indeed unfortunate, Madam, that my sonnet should so disappoint.

VADIUS:
> I should add, while it was being read, I was buzzed by a bumblebee,
> And the man in front was snoring, and his wife had a dreadful cough,
> So it is just possible I may have been more than a little distracted,
> And the chap who read it was not very good; I'm afraid he overacted,
> So—

TRISTAN:
> This is an outrage.

VADIUS:
> Sorry. It was not my intention to scoff.
> By way of compensation, please accept the gift of my ballad.

TRISTAN:
> Ballads are not to my liking; I find them insipid and rigid;
> They hail from a bygone era, and strike me as soulless and frigid.

VADIUS:
> I beg to disagree; it is a form that's stylistically valid.

TRISTAN:
> Ballads are for snobs and pedants;

VADIUS:
> Then it should appeal to you.

TRISTAN:
> Go back to your ivory tower, and let those of us who can, write.

VADIUS:
> One of my duties in the 'tower' is to expose plagiarism to the light.

ACT THREE

There is barely a phrase in your sonnet, which is either original or new.
You have plundered the works of others, creating a false impression,
Selling second-hand goods; you are a disgrace to your profession.
   VADIUS *goes, followed by* CLINTON.

SCENE FOUR

TRISTAN, PHILOMENA, AMANDA, JULIET.

TRISTAN:
None of that was true, Madam, and you mustn't blame me
For my anger at Doctor Vadius' attempts to shame me.
I was defending your good judgment of my sweet little sonnet.

PHILOMENA:
She herself openly admitted she had a bee in her bonnet.
Do not trouble yourself; professional envy is alive and well.
I will apply my healing powers to repair that unhappy quarrel.
But let's talk of another matter. Come here, Juliet.
For a rather long time, I have found it a cause of regret
That you don't seem to have a mind, and are vacuous; that said,
I have now discovered a way of installing one in your head.

JULIET:
You'd be going to a lot of trouble, and totally wasting your time.
I don't aspire to clever talk; there are no heights I wish to climb.
I like to live simply, and not stress over everything;
When I think of all the misery that growing a mind can bring,
I just don't have an ambition to mess about with my head.
I find I'm perfectly happy, Mama, to be blissfully stupid instead.
And things go much better for me if I use ordinary communication
Without jumping through rings of fire to make brilliant conversation.

PHILOMENA:
Yes, but I am wounded to the core, as it could never satisfy me
To suffer one of my bloodline bringing such shame and infamy;
The beauty of your face is but a fragile ornament,
A passing flower, a falling star that vanishes in the firmament;
Such beauty is only attached at best to a thin layer of skin,

But the mind is deep and intrinsic; unlike a face, it has no twin;
I have searched to find you that inner beauty which time cannot erode:
Some knowledge to penetrate your skull and take up ardent abode,
In the hope that thought might occur in that desert between your ears;
Well, finally I hit on the answer, which is one of my brightest ideas:
Namely, to attach you to a man who has a bountiful and fertile mind.
My choice is Tristan Tosser here; through him you'll become refined.
By determining that he be your husband, I've handed you a golden cup.

JULIET:
You don't mean me, Mama?

PHILOMENA:
                      Yes, of course, you. Do try to keep up.

TRISTAN:
In my ravishment, Juliet, the only thing I venture to say
Is that I see this marriage as the highest honour, and, if I may—

JULIET:
That's all very well, Monsieur, but this has not been settled yet.
So don't be so hasty—

PHILOMENA:
                    What a strange response, Juliet!
Surely you know that if—Oh never mind; you have heard me.
[*To* TRISTAN] Don't worry, she will see reason; and what I wish, shall be.

SCENE FIVE

JULIET, AMANDA.

AMANDA:
I think our mother is brilliant to have resolved what to do:
To find an illustrious poet as the perfect husband for you.

JULIET:
>If the choice is so brilliant, why don't you marry him yourself?

AMANDA:
>He was offered to you, not me.

JULIET:
>I worry you'll be left on the shelf,
>So I give him all to you, as you are my elder sister.

AMANDA:
>If mother made me so charming an offer, it would be hard to resist her;
>But as I don't agree with marriage, it would amount to a deception.

JULIET:
>Well, given your passion for pedants, surely you could make an exception?

AMANDA:
>Despite the fact that each of us has a very different taste,
>It's on our parents' will, not ours, that all such choices are based.
>A mother has power over us, and so at her insistence,
>One simply must obey; it's futile to offer resistance.
>Just so you know, she asked my opinion on who would be right for you,
>Of course I could have said Clinton, but I decided not to.
>Tristan seemed a better idea because, in all propriety,
>At least this marriage will establish you in educated society.

SCENE SIX

CHRISTOPHER, VADIUS, CLINTON, JULIET, AMANDA.

CHRISTOPHER:
>[*Presenting* CLINTON] Come here, Juliet, I need you to approve my plan;
>If you consider him your soul mate and the love of your life,
>Then remove your glove, my dear, and take the hand of this man,
>For it is my earnest wish that you should become his wife.

AMANDA:
>Sister, you look ecstatic! How crushing to have to say no.

JULIET:
A father has power over us, and so at his insistence
I will echo the advice that you gave me but a moment ago:
One simply must obey; it's futile to offer resistance.

AMANDA:
But a mother also has a part to play in our obedience.

CHRISTOPHER:
What on earth do you mean?

AMANDA:
                            You and mother have different views;
And therefore in this matter, I question your expedience;
Mother settled on another man;

CHRISTOPHER:
                            Be quiet! It's Clinton I choose!
If you want some half-baked Latin scholar, go and live in ancient Rome!
And stay out of our decisions, and this marriage, just for a start.
Go and play your bloody power games until the cows come home!
You might think your mind is alive, but you're totally dead in the heart!
Tell your mother that our daughter should marry out of love and respect!
And tell her there's no point at all in bending my bloody ear;
We must not let some pompous pedant treat our daughter with cold neglect!
We either make good decisions together, or I'll piss off out of here.
Well? What are you waiting for! Go on!

    AMANDA *goes.*

VADIUS:
                            That was good.

JULIET:
It was awesome!

CLINTON:
[*To* CHRISTOPHER] How lucky you spoke for us.

VADIUS:
                            Yes. Very wise.

CHRISTOPHER:
    Now then, take each other's hand, and stand here, if you would;
    Yes, I can see the happiness that shines inside your eyes.
    See her to her room, now.
      They go, stopping to kiss.
    [*To* VADIUS]   Ah! The sweet kisses of youth.
    Look at them together; it reminds me when I was a boy:
    I'll never forget falling in love, that summer of tender truth.
    This has really bucked me up, to witness this moment of joy.

END OF ACT THREE

ACT FOUR

SCENE ONE

AMANDA, PHILOMENA.

AMANDA:
Yes, nothing restrained her at all; she showed no equivocation,
In fact she made quite a display of her lack of hesitation.
She seemed in such a hurry to defy any obstruction
That she hardly had time to hear her father's instruction.
And it wasn't so much that she wanted to obey her father,
But more a case of whatever it takes to disobey her mother.

PHILOMENA:
Well, I'll show her a thing or two about whose rules she'll obey;
It's Reason she will submit to and its laws will hold sway.
She needs a harsh reminder to which parent she owes a duty,
She'll submit to the truth of the mind, not the whimsy of bodily
    beauty.

AMANDA:
At least they should ask your opinion, which they've chosen to
    ignore,
As that simple boy bullies his way into being your son-in-law.

PHILOMENA:
Well, he hasn't got there yet, and I assure you he's not about to;
I found him quite attractive, when he had his eye on you,
But his manners always displeased me; he knew my writing was
    divine,
Yet never once did he ask me to read him a single line.

SCENE TWO

CLINTON, AMANDA, PHILOMENA.

CLINTON *enters, unnoticed, during:*

AMANDA:
If I were in your position, Mama, I would never agree

ACT FOUR

To Juliet taking Clinton in this mismatched matrimony.
It would be quite unfair to suggest I bear malice under the surface,
Or that what I say is motivated by some ulterior purpose;
I know that by this low act, his intention is purely to vex me;
Far from being riddled with revenge, it's all too terrestrial to perplex me.
Against this barbarous treachery, my soul is well fortified
By the protective shield of philosophy, as over the sludge I glide.
But: To treat *you* in this manner is to push you towards an abyss
And take a sledgehammer to your honour; he mustn't get away with this.
He's just not your kind of son-in-law; we're talking about a man who,
Whenever we chatted together, never once spoke warmly of you.

PHILOMENA:
    The swine!

AMANDA:
          Some twenty times I read to him your finest writing;
He said that watching paint dry was twenty times more exciting.

PHILOMENA:
    The snake!

AMANDA:
          Whenever you were praised, his response was truly heinous;
He said that your hottest prose was 'as cold as a penguin's penis'.

PHILOMENA:
    The brute!

AMANDA:
          It gets worse: He said your posturing bordered on farce,
And went on to claim your pretension was, quote, 'a pain in the—'

CLINTON:
        Ah,
Sweet ladies, please! Go lightly! And give me a break!

[*To* AMANDA] A little honesty wouldn't go astray; I mean, for heaven's sake:
What wrong have I done to you? And what exactly is my offence?
Why take up arms against me in this torrent of eloquence?
And why do you want to destroy me, and go to so much pain
To diss me with the people whose support I need to gain?
So speak up, Mandy! Tell me the reason for this evil grudge.
[*To* PHILOMENA] As you are so fair-minded, Madam, I'd like you to act as judge.
I didn't say that bit about the penguin, or call you a pain in the—

AMANDA:
But the malice you accuse me of does not in fact reign in the
Heart, but if it did, I would have plenty of justification
And you would deserve every word of my fair condemnation,
Because First Love establishes a sacred claim over our soul
And one would sooner lose one's life and sink into a hole
Than try to love another man, after your First Love's rejection.
And it's an act of monstrous infidelity for a lover to shift his affection.

CLINTON:
What you call infidelity was me doing what you told me to.
It was because of your lofty pride that the distance between us grew.
And how could I offend you, when I was only obeying your orders
That your heart was a no-go zone, with strictly protected borders?
At first, I readily admit, I was totally head over heels,
For two years I burned for you, with increasingly passionate appeals.
There was no fuss I wouldn't go to, no favour I wouldn't perform.
There I was totally on fire, while you didn't crack lukewarm.
I sacrificed everything for you, but you were hostile to my advances,
So I transferred my love to your sister, where I seemed to have better chances.
And it worked. So you tell me, is it your fault or mine? Be fair:
Was my heart chasing a change, or was it you who was pushing me there?

ACT FOUR

AMANDA:
> What you call hostile was me rejecting your vulgarity,
> Between your idea of love and mine, there was considerable disparity.
> I tried to reduce your rabid passion to a kind of Platonic purity,
> Where the beauty of Perfect Love blossoms into full maturity.
> You seemed entirely lacking in the spiritual and mental resource
> Through which one distinguishes pure love from feral intercourse.
> You had no taste whatever for the sweet union of two hearts
> Unless it also involved the exploration of bodily parts.
> You did not know how to love by being intellectually close,
> So you opened your little toolbox and proceeded to be carnal and gross;
> And to sustain the fire I lit in your heart, you got it into your noodle
> That it meant marriage, children, a dog, a mortgage, the whole kit and caboodle.
> How sick is that! With love like yours, my life was bound to worsen
> Because it's impossible to be married and to remain a clever person.
> The physical has no role to play in the thinking woman's passion;
> This perfect flame will only unite hearts that rise above fashion.
> It only dwells in pure thoughts, it has no interest in sexual games,
> And nothing impure can survive the heat of this most sacred of flames.
> It is love for the sake of love, as if two holy fires have kissed.
> These delights are solely for the mind, as if the body doesn't really exist.
> All mundanities are left behind like so much flotsam and jetsam;
> You won't know this celestial fire until you get up, go out and get some.

CLINTON:
> Well, I'm sorry to disappoint you, but I'm a body as well as a soul
> And I'm equally attached to both as a kind of united whole.
> The dizzy heights of philosophy I don't pretend to understand,
> But I do know that my body and soul pretty much go hand in hand.
> True, there's nothing more beautiful, as you yourself have said,
> Than all those genuine feelings which we hold inside our head,
> Those tender little thoughts that bring two like minds together
> Like a horse and a carriage; like a hat and a feather,

Free from physical interaction; but, by way of rebuttal,
I have to say: Love that pure is, to me, way too subtle.
Okay, I am a bit gross, as you so politely put it,
I love with my whole self, which shouldn't surprise, should it?
Because that's how I like to *be loved*, i.e., with the entire person;
To make love to half a human sounds like a kind of perversion.
I mean, surely that kind of chastity can't be good for us, can it?
You might as well kiss a cadaver, if the sparkle has left the planet.
You're entitled to your opinion, weird and whacko as it may be,
But I have to tell you that the rest of the world pretty much agrees with me
That marriage is still in fashion, and it's a decent and loving bond,
And yes, I wanted to be your husband, but you failed to respond.
Your reasons for rejecting me were ethereal and extensive,
But it was never my intention to seem vulgar or offensive.

AMANDA:
Oh, well, little man!

CLINTON:
                Oh well, what, big woman?

AMANDA:
                                Oh well, now I see!
Since you obviously are determined not to listen to me,
You win! I will give in to your bestial inclinations
And your crude idea of faithful love with all its limitations.
I will succumb to the flesh, and anoint myself with unctions
And prepare to yield completely to all bodily functions.
If my mother gives me permission, I will overrule my mind
And agree to be your wife, leaving all misgivings behind!

CLINTON:
It's too late. The position's taken; I'm afraid you've been replaced,
And for me to return to you would show an appalling lack of taste,
I would never abuse the refuge that saved me from your cruel pride
By hurting Juliet's feelings; it is with her my heart will reside.

PHILOMENA:
But you would need to have my support, which I assure you, you don't.

ACT FOUR 67

So if you think you will marry Juliet, let me be clear: You won't.
In the midst of all your delusions, I consider it only fair
To tell you she'll marry Tristan; a fact of which you seem unaware.

CLINTON:
Oh, Madam, please change your mind! Don't inflict this indignation!
Don't plunge me into a living hell with so cruel a humiliation,
To see myself fall so low as to be Tristan Tosser's rival;
I know you worship writers, which works against my survival,
But when choosing my opponent, did you have to go as low as that?
He's so low he could walk under a snake while wearing a top hat.
Bad taste has a lot to answer for, treating him like Socrates
And calling such men genius, who in fact are mediocrities.
Tristan Tosser fools no-one; his writing is universally panned,
Apart from in this house, that is, and I fail to understand
How I must have heard twenty extracts fall from his lofty height
Which you elevate to heaven and which you beg him to recite
And you go on as if they're marvels, which you say are rightly acclaimed,
When I know that if you had written them you would be deeply ashamed!

PHILOMENA:
If you judge him so differently from the way in which we do,
Then it follows that we see him through different eyes than you.

SCENE THREE

TRISTAN, AMANDA, PHILOMENA, CLINTON.

TRISTAN:
I come to announce spectacular news, which has rendered me agape!
While we were asleep, Madam, we had a very narrow escape:
A comet, which was passing beside us, fell across our vortex
And came within dangerous proximity of our planet's outer cortex!
If, in its blazing trajectory, it had been unable to pass,
It would have collided with us, and shattered the Earth like glass!

PHILOMENA:
> How deeply discombobulating; but we must defer that conversation,
> As our friend here is utterly clueless on astrophysical devastation.
> He has no scientific curiosity, his mind being a vacuous chasm,
> And he cherishes his ignorance with disturbing enthusiasm.

CLINTON:
> Against this character assessment, I plead a right of reply:
> No-one respects knowledge and science more sincerely than I;
> In themselves, they are good and beautiful; no-one denies this;
> But when knowledge ruins people, then ignorance is bliss;
> I'd rather be completely ignorant, with all the shame it implies
> Than be like certain people, who know everything, but are not wise.

TRISTAN:
> I must say, for my part, that this argument rings feeble
> As I cannot imagine how knowledge could ever ruin people.

CLINTON:
> My point is: You have to look exactly where this knowledge leads;
> In the wrong hands, it can make great fools, both in words and deeds.

TRISTAN:
> That strikes me as a paradox.

CLINTON:
> Sorry, I didn't mean to be clever,
> But without much trouble I reckon I could prove this point, however,
> I couldn't give you actual reasons, or quote chapter and verse on this,
> But there are living examples of well-read fools who are hard to miss.

TRISTAN:
> You'd have to find a living example in order to prove your case.

CLINTON:
> Trust me: I don't have to go far before I'm looking one in the face.

ACT FOUR

TRISTAN:
    I myself don't observe these living examples you have in mind.
CLINTON:
    They stand out like balls on a camel; I mean, you'd have to be blind.
TRISTAN:
    I have believed all my life the doctrine one was taught at school,
    'Tis knowledge that maketh the wise man; 'tis ignorance that maketh the fool.
CLINTON:
    Well, you have believeth wrong, I'm afraid; 'tis something I can guarantee:
    A learnèd fool is more of a fool than an ignorant fool can be.
TRISTAN:
    I know not whence come your maxims; I suspect they must be anonymous,
    For the commonly held view is that '*ignorant*' and '*foolish*' are synonymous.
CLINTON:
    Oh, well, if you want to mince words, I'm not much of a debater,
    But the proximity between '*fool*' and '*pedant*' is actually even greater.
TRISTAN:
    Fools alone have foolishness.
CLINTON:
                                         And pedants are naturally pedantic.
TRISTAN:
    You cannot put a price upon knowledge, yet its value is gigantic.
CLINTON:
    But pedants are a dime a dozen, and you can get fools for the same rate.
TRISTAN:
    You must find ignorance very attractive to defend it as a noble state.
CLINTON:
    If for me ignorance is appealing, it's because every now and then,

    I have been exposed to certain charlatans, who are posing as Great
        Men.
    Between ignorance and pretension, I find ignorance the lesser
        crime;
    And when offered ignorance or arrogance, I'll take ignorance
        every time.
TRISTAN:
    Certain people may seem arrogant because of the disrespect we
        show them;
    They may be as good as certain others, if we bother to get to know
        them.
CLINTON:
    Yes, but if we rely on clever people to tell us who's clever,
    When clever people can't agree, then we won't know who's clever
        forever.
PHILOMENA:
    It seems to me, you upstart—
CLINTON:
                                God, I'm attacked on both flanks!
    Surely Tristan can look after himself, without bringing in the tanks.
    I already have a worthy opponent, and if I may be so blunt,
    Even I know from history not to fight a war on more than one front.
AMANDA:
    I have held back from this intense exchange, which I've heard in
        snatches—
CLINTON:
    And now more reinforcements! Quick! Batten down the hatches!
PHILOMENA:
    One can suffer some robust crossfire in any conversation
    As long as no-one in particular is the target of vilification.
CLINTON:
    My God! It's impossible to offend him; the man is immune from
        attack!
    Whenever he leaves an assembly, he cops a fresh load of arrows
        in his back.

ACT FOUR

    To suggest the man is sensitive is totally preposterous!
    He's an insult on legs, and has a hide like a rhinoceros!
TRISTAN:
    I am taken aback by this *affront* spoken right to my face,
    But I ignore, from this larrikin, a thesis so ignoble and base.
    He is 'a man of the people', and everybody's best friend.
    The people are his standard; above the mire no mind may ascend;
    They are the mob, which has a natural interest in promoting ignorance;
    This young man is its advocate, and thus takes up its defence.
CLINTON:
    You seem to have a bit of a thing about this unruly mob,
    Whose self-esteem is hardly helped by the put-downs of a snob;
    Every day, you treat the people like a bunch of clueless fools
    Who are the cause of all the problems that beset you born-to-rules.
    You accuse us of being philistines, who are a drain on the public purse;
    And we are somehow responsible for making your failures worse.
    Well permit me, Tristan Tosser, with all the respect you deserve,
    To tell you what you and your colleagues would do very well to observe:
    Stop treating the people with contempt; and take a more respectful tone;
    We're not as stupid as you think; good taste isn't yours alone,
    And we have enough common sense to know when you're pulling the wool.
    We are the spirit of the world, we've got goodwill by the bucketful,
    And if our earthy occupations are not sufficiently sedentary,
    It won't flatter you to know we beat the hell out of your pedantry.
TRISTAN:
    Was that outburst an illustration of your notion of good taste?
CLINTON:
    Perhaps you might enlighten me, in what way it was debased?
TRISTAN:
    Nowhere in your diatribe, Monsieur, did you bother to place

reliance
On a reference from literature or a principle of science.
Why? The answer's obvious: You're unaccustomed to such support,
When your standard of evidence is the mob rule of the people's court.

CLINTON:
Ah, I see your problem: I failed to refer to *your* writing;
Some juicy poetic extract might have made my case more exciting.
I momentarily forgot that the entire destiny of our nation
Rides upon your precious pen and its dazzling illumination.
My words are merely oral, but yours are published in print;
My opinions have little value, but yours are worth a mint.
Let universal glory now be crowned upon your head
For the simple reason you're able to quote from Great Men who are dead.
If you aspire to be the most learnèd of all, then go ahead and be it:
But remember that we, the unruly mob, know good writing when we see it!

PHILOMENA:
How dare you behave in this heated manner to our Writer of the Week!
Your true nature has been revealed in the insolent way you speak!
It is the good name of your rival here that prompts this jealous display!
And further proof my judgment is sound; and my daughter will obey—

SCENE FOUR

VADIUS, TRISTAN, PHILOMENA, CLINTON, AMANDA.

VADIUS *enters. She has books.*

VADIUS:
Please pardon me, Madam, in paying this unscheduled visit.

PHILOMENA:
You are always welcome, Doctor Vadius. Would you like a glass of water?

ACT FOUR

VADIUS:
>Tristan brags everywhere that he is going to marry your daughter,
>A claim I find disturbing for a very good reason.

PHILOMENA:
>What is it?

VADIUS:
>I have to warn you his true philosophy is to marry into your riches.
>And I strongly advise you to abandon the idea of him for your son-in-law.
>I am at present composing a statement, to reveal his true colours and more.
>But meanwhile, there's yet another purpose for my visit.

AMANDA:
>Which is?

VADIUS:
>Here is a copy of his sonnet, which Tristan says came from his soul ...

TRISTAN:
>Cease this vexatious annoyance! You have no right to barge in!

VADIUS:
>... And here are several books, where you'll see I've marked in the margin
>To show you the passages he plundered and the phrases that he stole.

TRISTAN:
>This is a slanderous libel, to announce this nonsense so zealously!

VADIUS:
>When you have had a chance to peruse these, then I bid you all
>To consider whether one word of the sonnet was in fact original.

>>AMANDA *looks through the books at the pages marked. She is gradually disturbed by them.* TRISTAN *angrily snatches a book from her.*

TRISTAN:
>I cannot brook these haughty menaces!

PHILOMENA:
                                                      As I said, it's professional jealousy.
You can see how this marriage, which I have decided upon
Is attacked by so many enemies, despite its obvious merit.
This ill feeling today is mischievous and I will not bear it.
I sniff my husband's paw in this, and will speak with him anon.
Unpleasantness before a wedding is the last thing we need.
The greater is the envy, the more confident I am to defeat it;
The more triumphant the enemy feels, the more determined I am to beat it.
These books, Doctor Vadius, are very impressive indeed;
I want you to know I place great value upon your impartial advice;
I knew Tristan to be an excellent scholar, but not that he was *that* good;
He's researched Catullus, Horace, Terrence, Virgil and Margaret Atwood.
You have convinced me to follow my instincts, and so, to be precise,
Tristan will marry my daughter, and he'll do so this very night.
[*To* CLINTON] Despite your appalling conduct, you are a friend of the family,
And so I invite you to attend the wedding as part of the assembly;
Amanda, go and fetch the Attorney and inform your sister.

AMANDA:
                                                                                                   Alright.

PHILOMENA:
And remind Juliet who rules the roost; I'm sure she will concur.
    PHILOMENA *goes*.

AMANDA:
I don't need to tell my sister; Clinton can tell her the news;
He'll no doubt run to her room, and urge her to rebel and refuse;
Why should she hear it from me? Let Clinton attend to her.

SCENE FIVE

AMANDA, CLINTON.

AMANDA:
It pains me to say, Clinton, that things are not going your way.
CLINTON:
Well, I'm going to work very hard, Mandy, to relieve you of that pain.
AMANDA:
But I fear that all your efforts might ultimately be in vain.
CLINTON:
Perhaps you will see your fear is groundless if true love wins the day.
AMANDA:
I wish that it were so.
CLINTON:
      Then I can rely on your support?
AMANDA:
I watched you just now with Tristan; I liked very much what I saw.
And then it occurred to me you could make a nice brother-in-law.
Yes, you have my full backing.
CLINTON:
      Thank you, you're a good sport.

SCENE SIX

CHRISTOPHER, VADIUS, JULIET, CLINTON.

CLINTON:
Without your help, Monsieur, I will be one unhappy man;
Your wife's determined to crush me; because of some crazy whim,
Her heart is set on Tristan;
CHRISTOPHER:
      That is a ridiculous plan!
She must be off with the pixies! What the hell does she see in him?
VADIUS:
He plundered some Roman poets, which somehow gives him the

edge.

CLINTON:
She insists he marry Jules and that they do so right here tonight.

CHRISTOPHER:
As early as tonight?

CLINTON:
Yes, tonight!

CHRISTOPHER:
Well, here is my pledge:
I will counteract this little plan; it will be tonight alright,
But the couple getting married will be you two instead.

JULIET:
But she's sent out for an Attorney to draw up the contract;

CHRISTOPHER:
I see;
Then I'll make sure I get there first and try to get in ahead.

CLINTON:
Amanda's had a kind of epiphany; she's thawed and isn't so icy.
Your wife told her to prepare Jules for Tristan, but she wouldn't.

CHRISTOPHER:
She's come to what's left of her senses! She knows who is master here!

CLINTON:
When it came to the crunch, what she thought she'd do, she couldn't.

CHRISTOPHER:
This will improve our chances and make our direction clear.
[*To* JULIET] Wait here till we return; I'll put an end to this family feud.
Come, my dear Athénaïs, and you too, my son-in-law.

JULIET:
For heaven's sake, keep my father in this buoyant and defiant mood!

VADIUS:
I am completely at your service.

JULIET:
                           Thank you!

VADIUS:
                           Well, what are friends for?

CLINTON:
[*To* JULIET] I can have all the help in the world, but most important is to have your love.

JULIET:
Nothing in the world is certain except the love I have for you.

CLINTON:
The only time I feel happy is when it's you I'm thinking of.

JULIET:
I would never marry Tristan, but what if they force me to?

CLINTON:
No force on Earth is great enough to replace our love with fear.

JULIET:
I will do everything in my power to honour our sweet bond;
And if, despite all my efforts, we should lose the battle here,
Then I'll retreat to some secluded place out in the world beyond,
For without your love, I lose the flame that makes me love my life.

CLINTON:
I hope the day never comes when you must prove your love that way!

JULIET:
Unless I can live with you alone, then I will be no man's wife.

CLINTON:
May the justice of heaven see us together when night falls on this day.

END OF ACT FOUR

ACT FIVE

SCENE ONE

JULIET, TRISTAN.

JULIET:
    About this marriage, on which it's clear my mother's mind is set,
    And which I notice is causing so much trouble in the house,
    I wanted to talk to you, Monsieur, if I may, *tête-à-tête*,
    In the hope you'll listen to reason. You see, if you're my spouse,
    The dowry you receive would increase your material worth.
    Just do the maths; that kind of wealth means a lot to a mere mortal,
    But is an insult to a philosopher like you because it's so down-at-earth,
    It follows that you would reject such riches with a dismissive chortle,
    Because you must renounce them not only in words but in action.

TRISTAN:
    Oh, absolutely; a tremendous income holds no charm for me,
    It's your radiant beauty and piercing eyes that give me satisfaction;
    Your grace and your character, in such voluptuous degree,
    Are the only treasures that inspire my tender love for you.

JULIET:
    I am greatly indebted to you for the generous sentiments you state;
    And for such a flattering admission, my humble thanks are due,
    But I deeply regret, Monsieur, that I cannot reciprocate.
    I respect you every bit as much as anyone could ever do,
    But as for being able to love you, I have a pretty major hurdle:
    A heart, as you would agree, cannot be shared by two;
    Such love, like sour milk, is very soon bound to curdle,
    And as Clint has won my heart, I reckon I'll go with him,
    Though you're much more classy, with a crockload of talent and learning;
    I'm probably making a huge mistake since my judgment is pretty grim;

I admit, in the choice of a husband, I'm not really very discerning,
And the forces of reason will no doubt curse me for this act of blindness,
But there you go.
TRISTAN:
                It seems to me that the gift of marrying you
Would deliver into my hands a heart of most excellent kindness
Which, though currently possessed by Clinton, will undergo a gradual coup
As with a thousand little charms, I will transfer that possession to me.
JULIET:
No you won't; my soul is given to my First Love, as I explained,
And none of your magic charms can change what the future will be;
I have been very direct with you; my candour is unrestrained
And my frank confession should not surprise or offend you in any way.
You think you are more deserving, but love's not a merit system;
It's partly whimsy, partly instinct, or something nice that he'll do or say.
If it were based on rational choice, common sense, experience or wisdom,
Then I would leap into your arms with wholehearted enthusiasm.
But it isn't; so you'll have to allow me to plunge into ardent folly.
How could you rush into marriage, as if driven by some violent spasm,
When the price of your bride's obedience is a life of melancholy?
A man ought not take a wife forced on him by parental choice;
It should disgust him that the one he loves must sacrifice her entire life
Because of some high-handed decision, in which he has no voice.
How utterly emasculating, to have your mother-in-law choose your wife.
I am begging you, Monsieur: Do not rely on the rigor of her rights,
But go and find your own bride, which should not prove a difficult

quest;
Blind Freddy can see that your heart is riddled with desirable delights.

TRISTAN:
In order for me to begin to comply with your audacious request,
You would have to change the laws of nature governing my soul;
At the very least, you would have to cease being so obviously adorable,
And desist from flaunting those electric eyes, which set off a cardio drum roll.

JULIET:
Oh, come off the grass! And cut the crap! This is totally deplorable!
You know lots of princesses you write to in your poetical dialogue!
You paint them as incredibly charming, and oozing with amorous ardour.

TRISTAN:
You speak as if life is a fairytale!

JULIET:
                              It is! So go kiss a frog.

TRISTAN:
In poetry it's my mind that speaks; to satisfy the heart is harder.
It is not I who falls in love with a princess, but the poet I'm writing about.
For me, there is only one love, and that is the adorable Juliet.

JULIET:
Oh, God give me strength!

TRISTAN:
                        If this offends you, then have no doubt
That my offence towards you won't come to an end just yet.
In fact, this fervour, which hitherto your eyes have chosen to ignore,
Consecrates to you a flame of eternal duration
Which no power on earth can extinguish, because it burns from the core,
And given that you, my beauty, reject my adoration,
Why should I refuse a mother's help to consummate my throbbing

ACT FIVE

flame?
Providing I can obtain the prize that I so dearly covet,
And thus end up having you, it matters not how I play the game.
JULIET:
Ah, but you overlook a risk; I wonder if you've thought of it?
It's what happens when you violate a woman's sense of honour
By forcing her into submission, despite her lack of contentment.
One day, while imprisoned in the life that's imposed upon her,
She's having a sad-on, on the sofa, her mind oozing resentment,
And resentment turns to revenge; be very afraid; it's a toxic brew.
TRISTAN:
There's nothing in what you've said that prompts me to change my mind.
Whatever is needed to meet a challenge, a philosopher is ready to do.
Reason has purged me of arguments that are weak, vulgar or unrefined.
It puts me above the kind of concerns that you just alluded to;
I am careful to avoid even the faintest shadow of tedium,
And things outside my control are simply not my responsibility.
JULIET:
I am truly delighted, Monsieur, that we have struck such a happy medium,
I had no idea that philosophy could provide such peace and tranquillity
In a situation which otherwise could prove an utter disaster.
Such singular strength of mind must be given its due prominence;
You need a wife who's a scholar, who can recognise you as master,
A wife with a fine mind to match your philosophical dominance,
And since, to tell the truth, I would not dare consider myself worthy,
I'll leave it to someone else to raise a fanfare to your glorious life
While I retreat modestly into one that's far more earthy;
So, *entre nous*, I renounce the joy of ever becoming your wife.

TRISTAN:
> You're going to find out very soon that this matter has been resolved,
> As the Attorney was sent for and is probably already here.

SCENE TWO

CHRISTOPHER, CLINTON, JULIET.

CHRISTOPHER:
> Ah, Juliet! Good to see you! Let me tell you what's involved;
> Come over here and prepare yourself for a ceremony, my dear,
> In which you'll submit to your father's wishes and marry this man,
> And at the same time teach your mother a lesson, one that she'll never forget.

JULIET:
> Your resolution is praiseworthy; keep it up and go through with your plan;
> Be firm in what you wish, and let there be no regret.
> And don't let your good nature be hit for six, when mother comes in to bat.

CHRISTOPHER:
> What, you think I'm a drongo?

JULIET:
>   May God preserve me, no!

CHRISTOPHER:
> I might look like a silly galah!

JULIET:
>   Father, I never said that.

CHRISTOPHER:
> You think I'm irrational and incompetent?

JULIET:
>   I've never remotely thought so.

CHRISTOPHER:
> At my age, don't I have the right to be master of my domain?

ACT FIVE

JULIET:
Of course.
CHRISTOPHER:
    I'm not some wombat your mother leads round by the nose.
There's plenty of lead in my pencil!
JULIET:
        And long may it remain!
CHRISTOPHER:
Too right. So what are you on about?
JULIET:
        Let's not come to blows.
CHRISTOPHER:
Well, I must say this is a bit rich talking to your father that way.
JULIET:
If I have in any way offended you, that was not my intention.
CHRISTOPHER:
In this house I think it fair that people honour what I say.
JULIET:
Very good, father.
CHRISTOPHER:
    Apart from me, no-one should receive this attention.
JULIET:
Yes, point taken.
CHRISTOPHER:
    Then don't forget who's chief inside these four walls.
JULIET:
How could I?
CHRISTOPHER:
    And I'm the one who decides what's right for my daughter.
If God wanted Adam to be under the thumb, he would have given Eve balls.

JULIET:
Who could disagree with that?
CHRISTOPHER:
                                    And that's why Eve was made shorter,
So when it comes to a daughter's marriage, I draw up to my full height
And I command you to marry this man, regardless of your mother's wish.
JULIET:
Okay, then, anything you say; it is, after all, your right.
I give in, and will obey you; and thank you—he is quite a dish.
CHRISTOPHER:
That settles that, then. Now let's see if my wife dares to rebel.
CLINTON:
Well, here she comes with the Attorney, so we'll find out soon enough.
CHRISTOPHER:
I need you to back me up. She can be scary.
JULIET:
                                              Very well.
Leave it to me, I'll egg you on, especially if the going gets tough.

SCENE THREE

PHILOMENA, AMANDA, TRISTAN, ATTORNEY, CHRISTOPHER, CLINTON, JULIET.

PHILOMENA:
Can you not change this awful legalese to a poetic contract?
ATTORNEY:
The wording is standard, Madam, and in every particular, exact.
I would look rather silly if I were to rewrite it all in verse.
PHILOMENA:
Well, it all seems so barbaric, and the syntax is plainly perverse.
Can't we convert the currency from francs into pure gold?
And 'dowry' is such a squalid word; won't you be a little bold

ACT FIVE

And express it in terms of talents, Roman annuities or daily bread?
And where it says 'the fifteenth day', I'd like 'The Ides of March'
    instead.
ATTORNEY:
Your unusual requests, Madam, place me in a difficult spot.
If I did all that, my colleagues would say I had lost the plot.
PHILOMENA:
It seems there's no escape then, from this rampant barbarity.
All elegance must be sacrificed in the interests of legal clarity.
ATTORNEY:
By the by, Madam, I have a letter here from Argante and Damon.
PHILOMENA:
Who are they?
ATTORNEY:
              They're your lawyers.
PHILOMENA:
                                It'll make no sense to a layman,

   CHRISTOPHER *takes it.*

It'll be some tiresome money matter; we've more important things
    at hand.
We need to give all our attention to this affair.
ATTORNEY:
                                    I understand.
PHILOMENA:
Go to the table, Madam, and fill in the marriage contract.
ATTORNEY:
Very well, yes, the contract. Who then, is the bride, in fact?
PHILOMENA:
The bride is my daughter.
ATTORNEY:
                      Good.
CHRISTOPHER:
                              Her name is Juliet.

ATTORNEY:
>Excellent. And her husband-to-be?

PHILOMENA:
>   The finest man I've met,
>Monsieur Tosser here is the husband I am giving to her.

CHRISTOPHER:
>And Monsieur Clinton here is the husband I wish to confer.

ATTORNEY:
>Two husbands!? There's an ancient precedent dating back to the Normans
>But it's long been outlawed as bigamy, even among the Mormons.

PHILOMENA:
>What is stopping you, Madam? Write Tristan Tosser there!

CHRISTOPHER:
>You'll do nothing of the kind! Put Clinton as husband and heir.

ATTORNEY:
>I'll put nothing until both of you make a mature judgment and agree
>On precisely which of these two gentlemen you want the groom to be.

PHILOMENA:
>Follow my directions, Madam; the choice of husband is mine!

CHRISTOPHER:
>Do precisely as I tell you, Madam, write my choice on the dotted line.

ATTORNEY:
>I cannot complete the contract until I know whose decision holds sway.
>So I wonder if you'd mind telling me which of you I should obey?

PHILOMENA:
>Who do you think? Don't cross me! Do I look like second fiddle, honey?

CHRISTOPHER:
>I will not allow someone to pursue my daughter only out of love for money.

ACT FIVE

ATTORNEY:
>Do you mind if I wait in the next room, while you sort out this affair?
>And when you've reached an agreement, I'll be ready for you in there.

She goes out.

PHILOMENA:
>Do you really imagine that Tristan here cares one jot about our wealth?
>A wise man has more worthy concerns than marrying a girl by stealth.

CHRISTOPHER:
>Anyway, Sweetie-Pie, I've made the decision on my son-in-law.

PHILOMENA:
>Shut up, Chris! You've said quite enough! I won't stomach this anymore!
>My final choice is Tristan! And that settles it once and for all.

CHRISTOPHER:
>Don't take that tone with me! The choice of husband is not your call.
>I am putting my foot down; so, dear heart, you're out of luck.

PHILOMENA:
>And just who do think you are, some Lord High Monkey Muck?

CHRISTOPHER:
>I'm Juliet's father!

PHILOMENA:
>>Ha! Some father!

CHRISTOPHER:
>>What's that supposed to mean?

PHILOMENA:
>Deciding to faint while she was being born is the most resolute you've been.

CHRISTOPHER:
>That's unfair! I'd been up all night!

PHILOMENA:
                                        Yes, and I'd been through two days of labour!
You had to be scraped up off the floor and carried home by a neighbour.

CHRISTOPHER:
Why do you think you have the right to assume full control of this place?

PHILOMENA:
The answer to that, buster, is staring you in what's left of your face.

SCENE FOUR

MARTINA, PHILOMENA, AMANDA, TRISTAN, CHRISTOPHER, CLINTON, JULIET.

MARTINA:
I'm back!

PHILOMENA:
                     Oh my God! What's that verbal slut doing here?

CHRISTOPHER:
She was an excellent employee, till you chose to interfere.
I decided to re-engage her, despite your gnashing teeth.
You might be top of the pile, but there are good people underneath.

MARTINA:
Yeah, bloody right. And I hear you two have chucked one almighty wobbly,
Which must be all about finding a husband for Juliet, prob'ly.

CHRISTOPHER:
Exactly.

MARTINA:
              Well, bugger me dead, Clinton is drop-dead gorgeous,
Why would ya refuse him? Ya know he's always adored youse.
I mean, like, anyway you look at him, even if it's just side-on,
Or if you only saw him upside down, he'd still give you a wide-on.
So why dump her with Tristan? He's a gold-digger and a sly cat;

ACT FIVE 89

I mean, take one look at the bastard; Imagine waking up next to that!
He'd be pulling his pud in Latin, and she'd block her ears with cotton wool,
And when he gets onto Greek princesses, he'd bore the arse off a Mallee bull.

CHRISTOPHER:
Well said.

PHILOMENA:
       Must one suffer this jabbering monkey till she runs out of puff?

MARTINA:
I mean, these preaching pedants! Well, I for one have had enough.
I've said it once, I've said it a thousand times, I want no scholar for my spouse;
A clever brain is not at all what's needed to run a house.
And books, I tell you, they breed like rabbits; books are really for suckers;
Stacked all over the floor, I mean, where are you going to put the fuckers?
The only type of scholar that I'd ever want my husband to be
Is a bloke who only reads one book, and that one book is me.
He won't know A from B—um, sorry about this, Missus,
But as for bookish pedants, Lord, what a dud lot this is.
Nice writing is one thing, but no matter what objections you throw at me,
If you want my opinion of Tristan Tosser, he's a blowfly at the picnic of poetry.

PHILOMENA:
Are you done? Has your vulgar diatribe finally come to a halt?

CHRISTOPHER:
She speaks honestly.

TRISTAN:
       Ad nauseam, ad infinitum—

MARTINA:
                      Add a pinch of salt.

PHILOMENA:
> Yes, well I'm going to cut short all this tiresome chatter
> And carry out my wishes and put an end to the matter!
> [*To* CHRISTOPHER] Juliet and Tristan will be joined in marriage right away!
> I've said it; I want it; I don't care what you have to say!
> If you promised to give her Clinton, give him to Amanda instead!

CHRISTOPHER:
> Well, that might be a solution, so we can put this affair to bed.
> [*To* JULIET] What do you think of that idea? Maybe it's the way to go?

JULIET:
> You must be joking!

CLINTON:
> Monsieur, how could you?!

CHRISTOPHER:
> I think the answer's no.

> *As* AMANDA *speaks,* CHRISTOPHER *opens the legal letter given him by the* ATTORNEY. *He reads.*

AMANDA:
> On reflection, it is a proposition that would please him, no doubt,
> But I might weary of his beauty and the intellectual drought,
> As the species of love I yearn for must be pure as the morning star,
> It lets us soar to heaven, to the realm where angels are;
> For what unites our souls is the substance which is pensive,
> And not the material love, which Descartes calls the 'substance extensive'.

CHRISTOPHER:
> I'm sorry to have to interrupt your enthralling prattle, my dear,
> But I have some rather painful news, conveyed by this letter here.
> It's from your attorneys, Philly—Argante and Damon.

PHILOMENA:
> Well, what?
> I can't think of anything important that would come from that lot.

ACT FIVE

CHRISTOPHER:
'Dear Madam, we refer to our recent letter setting down the date
For your action in Commercial Causes, but we're sorry to relate
That as you failed to appear, the action was struck out at great
  cost
And thus a case you should have won, you have very decidedly
  lost.'
My God! We've lost the case!

PHILOMENA:
                              Oh, don't be so silly, Chris;
There are far more pressing concerns than a trivial thing like this.
If only you could be like me, instead of getting into a state.

CHRISTOPHER:
'Your lack of attention to this affair has bankrupted your estate.
We enclose here a copy of all the orders of the court.'
Bankrupted! My God! I didn't expect a disaster of this sort.
'If you do not pay the costs, your home will be seized as well.
And we also inform you that, today, the stock market fell,
And though we advised in our letter about your foreign investment
  transaction,
You completely failed to respond with the required urgent action.'

MARTINA:
Was that the letter I gave youse, which you ripped up and chucked
  away?

PHILOMENA:
Stay out of this, you trollop; who cares what you have to say?

CHRISTOPHER:
Oh my God! In one fell swoop we lose everything we own!

PHILOMENA:
Oh, what a shameful outburst! So what if everything is blown?
A truly wise man would not be concerned about such change of
  fate;
So we've lost property and money, we still have spiritual weight;
Now do let's focus on this wedding and forget about all this fuss,
Anyway, Tristan has sufficient resources to look after all of us.

TRISTAN:
> No, Madam; please refrain from pressing my marriage to Juliet.
> Your family is firmly against me, and this would cause further upset,
> And philosophically speaking, although of course I will dearly miss you,
> I think harmony would be better served if I withdraw from forcing the issue.

PHILOMENA:
> This reflection seems rather sudden, Monsieur, and without a decent space,
> It seems to follow most rapidly upon our financial disgrace.

TRISTAN:
> I am worn down and finally defeated by this formidable resistance,
> I would rather retreat with grace, than push on with humiliating persistence.
> Though marriage is an important ambition, a poet is not ultimately driven
> By the desire to possess a heart which has not been willingly given.

PHILOMENA:
> What I thought was your glory was in fact an attempt to deceive;
> And I am able to see quite clearly what till now I've refused to believe.

TRISTAN:
> You can see me however you wish, I frankly couldn't care less,
> For I place little value on your opinion, and I must confess,
> I am not the sort of man who can suffer these egregious insults;
> Your house is a mockery, Madam, like a day care centre for adults.
> I deserve to be treated with higher regard as your intellectual superior
> Instead of wasting my time with people who are, in all respects, inferior.
> [*In Latin*] *Vale.*
>
> > *He goes.* PHILOMENA *is crushed. Her eyes gradually settle on* MARTINA.

ACT FIVE

PHILOMENA:
How, how did *you* ... see it?

MARTINA:
                See what, Missus?

PHILOMENA:
                            His mercenary soul,
And that his nobility was all a charade, like he was just playing a role?

MARTINA:
Some knowledge is got from living, Missus. That's all I can say.

PHILOMENA:
I've been instructed by false voices.

MARTINA:
                        You're a good woman, led astray.

CLINTON:
[*To* PHILOMENA] I can't pretend I'm a scholar, Madam, but I'd be honoured to share with you
Whatever destiny has in store, and to do what we have to do
To survive this situation, and though all I have to offer is me,
You're welcome to every penny I'll earn, if I can be part of your family.

PHILOMENA:
Your generosity is most charming; how on earth did I fail to see
That all the while my true son-in-law was standing in front of me?

CLINTON:
So that's a 'Yes'?

PHILOMENA:
                That's a 'Yes'! I—

MARTINA:
[*Indicating* CHRISTOPHER]   Er-hmm.

PHILOMENA:
                        That is, my husband and I
Have great pleasure in announcing a change of direction, whereby

We join together in blessing this union of our daughter, Juliet,
To the only worthy son-in-law that any of us have ever met—
JULIET:
No, Mother, stop! I'm sorry to say, but I have changed my mind.
CLINTON:
What are you saying, babe?
CHRISTOPHER:
                                      But what better husband could you find?
JULIET:
[*To* CLINTON] I know how little money you have, and how poor we will be;
I've always known that you would be the perfect husband for me;
But because I love you so very much, I thought that by becoming your wife
I would be able to give you security, and to improve your situation in life.
But now that our fortunes have changed to this drastic extremity,
I adore you way too much to inflict on you such calamity.
CLINTON:
The only destiny I want is you, no matter how the cards fall,
Because any destiny without you, is really no destiny at all.
JULIET:
When two people are in love, they always talk like this,
But let's avoid the anxiety that would ruin our marital bliss,
As nothing erodes a loving bond like struggling to make ends meet;
When you can't afford the basic needs, and end up on the street,
Each accuses the other and patience begins to wear thin,
And love is replaced by bitterness as harsh reality kicks in.
CHRISTOPHER:
Is our sudden poverty the only reason for your change of heart?
JULIET:
Why else would I leave a wonderful man I've loved from the very start?

ACT FIVE

CHRISTOPHER:
> Then let nothing stand in the way of the beautiful bond you share.
> The letter I read is a fake; I made up the entire affair.
> It was a strategy, a surprise attack; it was Doctor Vadius' idea,
> I wanted to set a trap, to make Tristan's true colours appear.
> To deceive my wife and family is not something I am above
> When desperate measures are needed, all at the service of love.

CLINTON:
> Praise the Lord!

PHILOMENA:
> I can't wait to see the look on that scoundrel's face,
> When word of his filthy greed gets out all over the place.
> What a fitting punishment, when he finds out he's been trounced
> And he sees with what triumphant joy this wedding is announced.

CHRISTOPHER:
> I always knew, I did, that these two would tie the knot.

AMANDA:
> It was only through my sacrifice that she has the man she's got.

PHILOMENA:
> I wouldn't call it a sacrifice; you are wed to your philosophy;
> Give them your blessing and crown their love with sisterly generosity.

AMANDA:
> Jules pretends to be clueless, but it turns out she's actually quite smart;
> And Clinton will always have a very special place in my heart;
> My one request is that, when sitting with pipe and slippers by the fire,
> He spare a thought for the older sister, who, for a moment, he did admire.

> CHRISTOPHER *takes* PHILOMENA*'s hand.*

CHRISTOPHER:
> Well, let's go and tell the Attorney, who must be at the end of her tether,
> That Love and Reason have joined forces …

PHILOMENA: … and reached a decision together.

They lead the company away.
Wedding dance. Curtain.

THE END

GRIFFIN THEATRE COMPANY
AND BELL SHAKESPEARE PRESENT

THE LITERATI
BY JUSTIN FLEMING AFTER MOLIÈRE'S LES FEMMES SAVANTES
27 MAY - 16 JULY

Director Lee Lewis
Designer Sophie Fletcher
Co-Composers & Sound Designers Max Lambert and Roger Lock
Lighting Designer Verity Hampson
With Caroline Brazier, Gareth Davies, Kate Mulvany, Jamie Oxenbould, Miranda Tapsell

SBW STABLES THEATRE
27 MAY - 16 JULY

Government Partners

Griffin acknowledges the generosity of the Seaborn, Broughton and Walford Foundation in allowing it the use of the SBW Stables Theatre rent free, less outgoings, since 1986.

PLAYWRIGHT'S NOTE

We live in an age of spin. And so did Molière. The spin doctors may change in wardrobe, manners or language, but they remain a rich field for biting satire. That the learned fool is more of a fool than an ignorant one remains as much a conundrum for us in the 21st century as it did for audiences in the 17th. Molière wrote on the threshold of the Age of Reason, so any spin that amounted to nonsense on stilts was both repugnant and laughable.

I think Molière's work is principally about extremes. Such human forces as love, passion, honesty, health, money, authority and religion (even if it is an obsession with books) are better lived in the moderate zones. As soon as we traverse that corridor, especially if we try to drag everyone else with us, we are on the path to the destruction of happiness.

The Literati is many things, not least a piss-take on pretentious literary conceit, and as I approached the work, I always kept in mind some of the gushing hyperbole that passes for writers' festivals and book clubs both on television and off. In this vein, the play had a modern resonance, which I was eager to capture. Molière's title *Les Femmes Savantes* did not embrace the wonderful wankery of Tristan Tosser (Molière's Trissotin – his pun on three fools in one man). Hence, when Lee Lewis and Peter Evans asked me to find an appropriate all-inclusive title, I suggested *The Literati*.

Though Molière used rhyming couplets throughout, his audience was used to them, and in French, because of the frequent similar endings of words, they have less intensity. For variety's sake, and to give themes their breathing space, in scenes on lofty pretentiousness, I have used the rhyming couplets (AABB). When the subject is love, the rhymes are on alternate lines (ABAB). And for wisdom and true scholarship, the rhymes fall on the first and fourth lines, and the second and third lines (ABBA). I first experimented on this pattern with *Tartuffe* and remain grateful to director Peter Evans, the actors and audiences who so happily ran with it.

Justin Fleming
Writer

DIRECTOR'S NOTE

Molière at Griffin. *Qu'est-ce que c'est?* Griffin, the only theatre company in the country dedicated to the production of new Australian plays, producing an adaptation of a French classic ... is it all downhill into an international quagmire from here? *Mais non, mes amis! Calmez-vous.*

Justin Fleming has been in a serious literary relationship with Molière for many years now. I admired his work in a Peter Evans production at MTC in *Tartuffe* years ago. I directed his translation of *The School For Wives* in a production which toured around the country with Bell Shakespeare. I giggled helplessly at Kate Mulvany in another Evans Bell production of his *Tartuffe* at the Opera House in 2014. I witnessed his first draft of *Les Femmes Savantes* come to life in a reading for The Lysicrates Prize. Finally I realised that Justin is more than a translator of Molière (a difficult enough task in and of itself). He has become an Australian adaptor, interpreter, suggester and massager of Molière's original works to such an extent that, while remaining faithful to Molière's structures and stories, he is creating Australian versions that speak directly to Australian audiences about our own foibles here and now. These are not versions written for a relationship with a French audience. These are not versions that belong on the British stage or the American stage. They belong here.

So his work, his skill, his talent needs to be shown on the Griffin stage.

And it is enormous fun. Not to make. Comedy is horrifically hard. Verse comedy is hellishly impossible. Jammed into the tiny Stables space is the stuff of nightmares. With only five actors it is just ridiculous. Even when they are as good as this bunch. All of which possibly make Peter Evans and me the most foolhardy Artistic Directors in the country. But we both believe in Justin Fleming. And we both believe that if we can make it work, it will be enormous fun ... for the audience.

So the country's national classical company is teaming up with the country's new writing company to create a production of such linguistic dexterity, of such audaciously silly virtuosity that it will inspire playwrights around the country to dare more with their double entendres, to leap further in their language play, to bathe in the voluptuosity of verse, and ultimately to make people laugh.

So don't worry. We are still Australia's new writing theatre. Always have been. Always will be. It's just that the idea of what is an Australian play is evolving. In front of your eyes. I dare you to sit in the front row.

Lee Lewis
Director

ABOUT GRIFFIN THEATRE COMPANY

For nearly 40 years, Griffin has been dedicated to bringing the best Australian stories to the stage. We have a passion for developing Australian talent, with many of our nation's most celebrated artists starting their professional careers with us.

Griffin is a major force in shaping the future of Australian theatre: it is a home for the courageous and the curious, for the imaginations that inspire us. Iconic Australian stories such as *Lantana*, *The Boys*, *Holding the Man* and *The Heartbreak Kid* had their world premieres at Griffin.

Griffin produces an annual subscription season of four to five Main Season shows by Australian playwrights, and co-presents a season of new work with leading independent artists and special events from producers around the country. We also support artists through professional development opportunities, artist residencies and masterclasses.

Our home is the historic SBW Stables Theatre, Sydney's most intimate and engaging space for writers, actors and audiences to meet. We hope to see you here soon.

GRIFFIN THEATRE COMPANY
13 CRAIGEND ST
KINGS CROSS NSW 2011

02 9332 1052
INFO@GRIFFINTHEATRE.COM.AU
GRIFFINTHEATRE.COM.AU

SBW STABLES THEATRE
10 NIMROD ST
KINGS CROSS NSW 2011

BOOKINGS
GRIFFINTHEATRE.COM.AU
02 9361 3817

Justin Fleming
Playwright

Justin Fleming's plays include: for ATYP and Bakehouse Theatre Company: *His Mother's Voice*; for Belvoir: *Burnt Piano* (later produced by: Melbourne Theatre Company, Centaur (Montréal), Herbert Berghof Theater New York); for Courtauld Institute, London: *Origin* (later produced by Art Gallery of New South Wales); for Ensemble Theatre and Festival of Sydney: *Hammer*; for Melbourne Theatre Company: *Coup D'Etat* (later produced by: Bakehouse Theatre Company, Western Canada Theatre); for New York Ensemble Studio Theatre and Alfred P Sloan Foundation: *Soldier of the Mind*; for Old Fitz Theatre: *The Department Store*; for Riverside Theatres: *Shellshock*; and for Sydney Theatre Company: *The Cobra, Harold In Italy, The Ninth Wonder*. Justin's previous translations of Molière include: for Bell Shakespeare: *The School for Wives*; and for Melbourne Theatre Company: *Tartuffe (The Hypocrite)* (later produced by Bell Shakespeare). Justin's credits as librettist include: for Griffin, Wayne Harrison, Ross Mollison and Robert C Kelly: *Satango*; for Compact Opera (UK Tour) and Sadler's Wells: *Crystal Balls*; for Ensemble Theatre: *Ripper: The Terror of Whitechapel*; and for Savoy Theatre: *Tess of the D'Urbervilles*, which then toured the UK. Justin is also the author of *Stage Lines – Writing Scripts for the Stage*, published by Phoenix Education.

Lee Lewis
Director

Lee is the Artistic Director of Griffin Theatre Company and one of Australia's leading directors. Her directing credits for Griffin include: *The Bleeding Tree, The Bull, The Moon and the Coronet of Stars, The Call, Emerald City, A Hoax, Masquerade* (co-directed with Sam Strong), *The Nightwatchman, A Rabbit for Kim Jong-il, Replay, The Serpent's Tabl*e (co-directed with Darren Yap) and *Silent Disco*; for Bell Shakespeare: *The School for Wives, Twelfth Night*; for Belvoir: *That Face, This Heaven*; for Melbourne Theatre Company: David Williamson's *Rupert*, which toured to Washington DC as part of the World Stages International Arts Festival and to Sydney's Theatre Royal in 2014; and for Sydney Theatre Company: *Honour, Love Lies Bleeding* and *ZEBRA!*.

Sophie Fletcher
Designer

Sophie's theatre credits include, as Set and Costume Designer: for Griffin: *Caress/Ache, Emerald City*; for Belvoir: *This Heaven*; and for Pants Guys / ATYP: *Sweet Nothings*. As Design Assistant: for Belvoir: *Babyteeth, Every Breath, Peter Pan*; for Melbourne Theatre Company: *Miss Julie*; for Opera Australia: *The Marriage of Figaro, The Ring Cycle*; and for Sydney Theatre Company: *Gross und Klein, The Maids, Waiting for Godot*. Her film credits include, as Costume Designer: for Whitefalk Films: *Florence Has Left the Building*; as Production Designer: for Whitefalk Films: *Shadow Self*; and as Production and Costume Designer: for Whitefalk Films: *How to Get Clean*.

Max Lambert
Co-Composer & Sound Designer

Max is one of Australia's most talented composers, arrangers, musicians and musical directors. Composing credits include work for Sydney, Melbourne and Queensland Theatre Companies, Sydney Dance Company and The Australian Ballet. Recording album credits include: Kate Ceberano, Wendy Matthews, Grace Knight, Vince Jones, Renee Geyer, Paul Kelly, Iva Davies and Icehouse. Max's film credits include: George Miller's *Happy Feet*; Gillian Armstrong's *The Last Days of Chez Nous*. His musical theatre credits include, David Atkins' *Hot Shoe Shuffle*. Max's Musical Directorship credits include the Opening and Closing Ceremonies of *Sydney 2000 Olympic Games*; *2002 Commonwealth Games* (Manchester); and the *2006 Asian Games* (Doha, Qatar). His Musical Supervisor credits include: ARIA award-winning production *The Boy From Oz*, *Hairspray*, *Fame*, *King Kong* and *Strictly Ballroom the Musical*. The revival of Max's musical *Miracle City* (co-written with Nick Enright) was a runaway success at The Hayes Theatre in 2014. He is thrilled to be back at the SBW Stables working again with Roger Lock, having just worked as Composer and Sound Designer on Alana Valentine's *Ladies Day*.

Roger Lock
Co-Composer & Sound Designer

Guitarist, producer and composer Roger Lock studied guitar, composition and music technology at the Mozarteum University of Salzburg. As a concert guitarist he has played concerts in Austria, Germany, Italy, Sweden, Spain, Hungary and Taiwan before moving to Vienna in 2007. He has been very active as a concert and recording artist, producing albums with Dr. Opin, Eminence Symphony Orchestra, Yorgos Nousis, Laetitia Ribeiro, Jane Rosenson, Emma Sholl, Troebinger and his band project Roger Vs. The Man. He has taught at many tertiary institutions including the Sydney Conservatorium of Music and currently runs the Cranbrook Recording Studio. Roger is honoured to be back at Griffin after being the Associate Sound Designer on *Ladies Day*, and is delighted to be working with Lee Lewis and Max Lambert again.

Verity Hampson
Lighting Designer

Verity's previous theatre credits for Griffin include: *Beached, The Bleeding Tree, The Boys, The Bull, The Moon and the Coronet of Stars* and *The Floating World*. She is a NIDA graduate with over ten years' experience as a lighting and projection designer. She has designed for over one hundred theatre productions working with some of Australia's most talented directors and choreographers. Verity's television credits include: for ABC: *Live at the Basement* and *The Roast*. Verity was awarded the Mike Walsh Fellowship in 2012, which took her to Broadway to work with Tony Award-winning projection design company 59 Productions. She was also the winner of the 2013 Sydney Theatre Award for Best Mainstage Lighting Design for her work on *Machinal* at Sydney Theatre Company.

Charlotte Barrett
Stage Manager

Charlotte's previous stage management credits include: for Griffin: *A Rabbit for Kim Jong-il*; for Force Majeure: *Jump First, Ask Later, Nothing to Lose*; for Matthew Management & Neil Gooding Productions: *Thank You For Being A Friend*; for The National Theatre of Parramatta: *Swallow*; for Queensland Theatre Company: *Mountaintop, Stradbroke Dreamtime* (remount), *Youth Ensemble Showcase 2013*; for Queensland Theatre Company and Sydney Theatre Company: *The Effect*; and for Sydney Theatre Company: *Battle of Waterloo, The Golden Age*. Charlotte has also worked extensively as an Assistant Stage Manager: for Black Swan State Theatre Company and Queensland Theatre Company: *Gasp!*; for Opera Queensland: *The Perfect American*; for Queensland Theatre Company: *Macbeth, Other Desert Cities*; and for Shake & Stir Theatre Company: *Animal Farm* (Queensland Regional Tour).

Caroline Brazier
Philomena / Vadius

Since graduating from NIDA in 1998, Caroline Brazier has enjoyed an extensive career in film, theatre and television. Caroline's theatre credits include: for Bell Shakespeare: *Antony and Cleopatra, Julius Caesar, The Merchant of Venice*; for Critical Stages and Tamarama Rock Surfers: *I Want to Sleep with Tom Stoppard*, for which Caroline won a Sydney Theatre Award and a Glug Award for Best Actress in a Leading Role; for Melbourne Theatre Company: *Enlightenment, Jumpy, Ray's Tempest*; and for Sydney Theatre Company: *Don's Party*. Her television credits include: for ABC Studios/Paperboy Productions/Renaissance Pictures: *Legend of the Seeker*; for Amblin Television/Chernin Entertainment/Kapital Entertainment/Siesta Productions/20th Century Fox Television: *Terranova*; for Blow by Blow Productions/Essential Media: *Rake*, for which Caroline received an Equity Ensemble Award for Outstanding Performance for her role of Wendy Greene; for Endemol Australia: *Water Rats* (Nine Network), *Wild Boys* (Channel 7); for Every Cloud Productions: *Miss Fisher's Murder Mysteries* (ABC); and for Spectrum Films: *Packed to the Rafters* (Channel 7).

Gareth Davies
Tristan Tosser

This is Gareth's first production with Griffin. His previous theatre credits include: for Bell Shakespeare: *As You Like It*; for Belvoir: *As You Like It, Cat on a Hot Tin Roof, Peter Pan, The Seagull*; for Belvoir and The Hayloft Project: *The Only Child, The Suicide*; for Belvoir and Arts Radar: *Midsummer Night's Dream*; for Malthouse Theatre: *The Government Inspector* and for Melbourne Theatre Company: *The Cherry Orchard*. Gareth has also been involved in a number of works which he both devised and performed in: for Belvoir: *And They Called Him Mr Glamour*, which Gareth wrote; for Redline Productions: *Masterclass, Masterclass 2 - Flames of the Forge*, which he co-wrote with Charlie Garber; and as a member of Melbourne's Black Lung Theatre: *Avast* and *Avast II* (with Malthouse Theatre), *Doku Rai* (with Darwin Festival), *I Feel Awful* (with Queensland Theatre Company), *Pimms, Rubeville* and *Sugar*. Gareth appeared in the film *The Daughter* for Screen NSW and Fate Films. His television credits include: for Universal Cable Productions and Valhalla Entertainment: *Hunters*; and for Giant Dwarf: *The Letdown* (ABC).

Kate Mulvany
Amanda

Kate is one of Australia's most multi-talented and versatile artists. She has performed widely across stage, screen and television, and has written and produced over 25 plays and screenplays. As an actor, her theatre credits include: for Griffin: *Beached*; for Griffin and Riverina Theatre: *Mr Bailey's Minder*; for Bell Shakespeare: *Julius Caesar, Macbeth,* and *Tartuffe*, for which she received a Sydney Theatre Critics Award for Best Actress; for Belvoir: *Buried Child*; for Melbourne Theatre Company: *The Beast;* for Perth Theatre Company: *Amadeus, Milk & Honey, Social Climbers, Sweet Phoebe*; for Sydney Theatre Company: *A Man With Five Children, The Crucible, Festen, King Lear, Proof* and *Rabbit*. Kate's feature film credits include: *The Final Winter, Griff the Invisible,* Baz Luhrmann's *The Great Gatsby* and *The Turning*. Television credits include: *The Chaser's War On Everything, Chandon Pictures, Miss Fisher's Murder Mysteries, My Place, The Underbelly Files: The Man Who Got Away* and *Winter*. As a writer, some of Kate's original plays include: for Black Swan State Theatre Company and Hothouse Theatre: *The Web*; for Belvoir: *Jasper Jones, Medea* and *The Seed* – which, after several acclaimed seasons, is in development to become a feature film. She has also written a number of musicals including: for The Q Theatre Company: *Somewhere – The Magical Musical of Penrith* (co-written with Tim Minchin) and for the State Theatre Company of South Australia and Griffin Theatre Company: *Masquerade*. Kate has been a proud member of Actors Equity since 1997.

Jamie Oxenbould
Christopher/Clinton

Jamie has worked in the performing arts for over 25 years. His theatre credits include: for Griffin Independent and Apocalypse Theatre Company: *The Dapto Chaser*; for Darlinghurst Theatre Company: *Good Works*; for the Ensemble Theatre: *Chapter Two, Casanova, Fully Committed, Last of the Red Hot Lovers, Neighbourhood Watch, Seven Stories, The Spear Carrier* (one man show), *When Dad Married Fury*; and for Sydney Theatre Company: *The Tempest*. His television credits include: for ABC: *My Place, Playschool*; and for Yoram Gross: *Flippa & Lopaka*. Jamie also writes and directs short films. His films have screened at various film festivals including Adelaide Film Festival, Flickerfest, LA Shorts Festival, St Kilda Film Festival, the Tasmanian Breath of Fresh Air Film Festival (BOFA) and Tropfest.

Miranda Tapsell
Juliet / Martina

Miranda Tapsell is a proud Larrakia Woman from Darwin who grew up in Kakadu National Park. Her theatre credits include: for Belvoir: *A Christmas Carol, Radiance* and *Yibiyung*; for Riverside Theatres: *Rainbow's End*; for Sydney Theatre Company: *The Secret River*, for which she received a Helpmann Award nomination for Best Female Actor in a Supporting Role; for Sydney Festival: *I Am Eora*; for Yirra Yaakin Theatre Company: *Mother's Tongue*. Miranda appeared in the multi-award winning feature film, *The Sapphires*. Her previous television credits include: for ABC: *Black Comedy, Playschool, Redfern Now* and *Splash Content*; for Blackfella Films: *Mabo*; for Channel 9: *Love Child*, for which she won both the Most Popular New Talent and The Graham Kennedy Award for Most Outstanding Newcomer logies; for Foxtel: *Who We Are* (Season 3). Her upcoming television credits include: for ABC: *Cleverman* and *Maurice's Big Adventure*; for Foxtel: *Secret City*; for Screentime: *Wolf Creek*.

STAFF

Patron
Seaborn, Broughton and Walford Foundation

Griffin acknowledges the generosity of the Seaborn, Broughton and Walford Foundation in allowing it the use of the SBW Stables Theatre rent free, less outgoings, since 1986.

Board
Bruce Meagher (Chair), Sophie McCarthy (Deputy Chair), Tim Duggan, Patrick Guerrera, Lee Lewis, Kate Mulvany, Mario Philippou, Sue Procter, Lenore Robertson, Simone Whetton

Artistic Director & CEO
Lee Lewis

Associate Artist
Ben Winspear

General Manager
Karen Rodgers

Associate Producer - Programming
Melanie Carolan

Associate Producer - Development
Will Harvey

Associate Producer - Marketing
Estelle Conley

Publicist
Dino Dimitriadis

Communications Associate
Aurora Scott

Marketing & Administration Coordinator
Lane Pitcher

Strategic Insights Consultant
Peter O'Connell

Production Manager
Damien King

Production Coordinator
Daniel Barber

Financial Consultant
Tracey Whitby

Financial Manager
Kylie Richards

Technologist
Daniel Andrews

Customer Relations Manager
Elliott Wilshier

Box Office Coordinator
Nicola James

Front of House Manager
Damien Storer

Front of House
Renee Heys, Julian Larnach, Kristina Paraschos

Studio Artists
Sofya Gollan, Catherine Fargher & Heather Grace Jones, Sheridan Harbridge, Phil Spencer

Writers Under Commission
Mary Rachel Brown, Declan Greene, Michele Lee, Steve Rodgers

Web Developer
Holly

Brand and Graphic Design
RE:

Cover Photography
Brett Boardman

GRIFFIN DONORS

Income from Griffin activities covers less than 40% of our operating costs – leaving an ever increasing gap for us to fill through government funding, sponsorship and the generosity of our individual supporters. Your support helps us bridge the gap and keep ticket prices affordable and our work at its best. To make a donation and a difference, contact Griffin on 9332 1052 or donate online at griffintheatre.com.au

SEASON DONORS

Studio Program
Gil Appleton
James Emmett & Peter Wilson
Limb Family Foundation
Peter Graves
Sophie McCarthy & Antony Green
Rhonda McIver
Geoff & Wendy Simpson
Danielle Smith

Commission $12,500+
Darin Cooper Foundation
Anthony & Suzanne Maple-Brown

Main Stage Donor $5,000 - $10,000
The Sky Foundation
Peter Graves
Abraham James

Workshop Donor $1,000-$4,999
Anonymous (5)
Dr Gae Anderson
Ellen Borda
Jane Bridge
Alex Byrne & Sue Hearn
Richard Cottrell
Ros & Paul Espie
John & Libby Fairfax
Jono Gavin
Larry & Tina Grumley
Judge Joe Harman
James Hartwright & Kerrin D☐Arcy
Libby Higgin
Margaret Johnston
Richard & Elizabeth Longes
Elaine & Bill McLaughlin
Dr Stephen McNamara
Ian Neuss & Penny Young
Martin Portus
Sue Procter
Pip Rath & Wayne Lonergan
Merilyn Sleigh & Raoul de Ferranti
Mike Thompson
Jane Thorn
Adrian Wiggins & Siobhan Toohill
Paul & Jennifer Winch

Reading Donor $500-$999
Anonymous (4)
Wendy Ashton
Melissa Ball
Angela Bowne
Bernard Coles
Bryony & Tim Cox
Fiona Dewar
Max Dingle
Wendy Elder
Jacqueline Hayes
Angela Herscovitch
Michael Hobbs
Susan Hyde
C John Keightley
Daniel Knight
John Lam-Po-Tang
Jennifer Ledgar & Bob Lim
Rebecca Macfarling & Paul Warnes
Lisa Manchur
Carina Martin
John McCallum
Dr Wendy Michaels
Anthony Paull
Steve & Belinda Rankine
Alex Oonagh Redmond
Karen Rodgers & Bill Harris
Diana Simmonds
Catherine Sullivan & Alexandra Bowen
Isla Tooth
Judy & Sam Weiss
Simone Whetton

First Draft Donor $200-$499
Anonymous (4)
Priscilla Adey
Jes Andersen
Robyn Ayres
Pamela Bennett
Julie Bridge
Rob Brookman & Verity Laughton
Wendy Buswell
Bryan Cutler
Eric Dole
Susan Donnelly
Tim Duggan
Michele Dulcken
Elizabeth Evatt
Corinne & Bryan Everts
Michael & Kerrie Eyers
Matt Garrett
Sheba Greenberg
Jennifer Hagan
Ross Handsaker
Elizabeth Hanley
Will Harvey & Ester Harding
John Head
Janet Heffernan
Danielle Hoareau
Mary Holt
Val Jory
Ross Kelly
Carolyn Lowry
Ian & Elizabeth MacDonald
Rob Macfarlan & Nicole Abadee
Stephen Manning
Christopher McCabe
Patrick McIntyre
Duncan McKay
Nicole McKenna
Kent Carrington McPhee
Keith Miller
Sarah Miller
Neville Mitchell
Kate Mulvany
Kerry O☐Kane
Annie Page & Colin Fletcher
Mario Philippou
Crispin Rice
Rebecca Rocheford Davies
Ellen & Trevor Rodgers
Julie Rosenberg
Catherine Rothery
Dianne & David Russell
Gemma Rygate
Julianne Schultz
Roger Sewell
Jann Skinner
Geoffrey Starr
Augusta Supple
Sue Thomson
Benson Waghorn
Arisa Yura
William Zappa
Aviva Ziegler

We would also like to thank Peter O☐Connell for his expertise, guidance and time.

Current as of 05/04/2016

PRODUCTION DONORS

You made this.

Production donors make a direct contribution to the costs of staging an individual play, chosen for its unique voice and the strength, insight and candour it brings to the stage. For more information, please contact our Development Manager on 9332 1052.

LADIES DAY 2016

Production Patrons
Robert Dick & Erin Shiel
Reay McGuinness
Richard McHugh
& Kate Morgan
Bruce Meagher
& Greg Waters
Richard Weinstein
& Richard Benedict

Production Partners
Cambridge Events
Michael Hobbs
Steve Riethoff
Annabel Ritchie
Diana Simmonds
Jenny & Peter Solomon

THE BLEEDING TREE 2015

Presenting Partner
Gil Appleton

Production Patrons
Peter Brereton
Robert Dick & Erin Shiel
Richard McHugh
& Kate Morgan
Richard Weinstein
& Richard Benedict

Production Partners
Tina & Maurice Green
Jon & Katie King
Bruce Meagher
& Greg Waters
John Mitchell
Rachel Procter
Steve Riethoff
Simone Whetton
Carole & David Yuile

GRIFFIN FUND

Griffin Fund Donors
Anonymous (1)
Baly Douglas Foundation
John Bell & Anna Volska
Nathan Bennett & Yael Perry
Michael & Charmaine Bradley
Ange Cecco & Melanie Bienemann
Alison Deans & Kevin Powell
Catherine Dovey & Kim Williams
Lilian & Ken Horler
Peter Ingle
Kiong Lee & Richard Funston
Lee Lewis & Brett Boardman
Sophie McCarthy & Antony Green
Bruce Meagher & Greg Waters
Dr David Nguyen
Peter & Dianne O'Connell
Ian Phipps
Ian Robertson
Will Sheehan
Stuart Thomas
Simon Wellington & Sanjeev Kumar
Carole & David Yuile

GRIFFIN SPONSORS

Griffin would like to thank the following:

Government Supporters

Patron

2016 Season Sponsor

Production Sponsors

Foundations and Trusts

Company Lawyers

Associate Sponsor

Company Sponsors

Griffin Theatre Company is assisted by the Australian Government through the Australia Council, its arts funding and advisory body; and the NSW Government through Arts NSW.

ABOUT BELL SHAKESPEARE

"We know what we are, but know not what we may be." Hamlet

Since 1990 Bell Shakespeare has firmly established itself as Australia's only truly national theatre company, taking the immortal plays of William Shakespeare and peers such as Marlowe, Jonson and Molière to all corners of Australia, appearing on stages, in schools and in regional and remote communities nationwide.

Over the decades, some of the greatest directors, actors and artists in Australian theatre have proudly contributed their talents to the company's mainstage and education programmes, helping to produce an unrivaled body of work that has engrossed, inspired and stimulated audiences across the entire nation.

Originally under the guiding hand of Founding Artistic Director, John Bell AO, and now helmed by Artistic Director Peter Evans, Bell Shakespeare's core mission remains the same as it was in 1990; to reinterpret the beautiful words, complex themes, raw emotions and profound ideas found in each Shakespeare play and show their relevance for modern Australians - wherever they live and whatever their background.

We heartily thank the Darin Cooper Foundation and Kathryn Greiner AO for their support of The Literati Syndicate.

BELL SHAKESPEARE
LEVEL 1, 33 PLAYFAIR STREET
THE ROCKS NSW 2000
PO BOX 10
MILLERS POINT NSW 2000

T +61 2 8298 9000
E MAIL@BELLSHAKESPEARE.COM.AU
BELLSHAKESPEARE.COM.AU

BELL SHAKESPEARE DONORS

Supporting Cast

Bell Shakespeare is incredibly grateful for every dollar our Supporting Cast donors contribute towards our essential operating costs, ensuring that we're able to focus our efforts on finding new ways to educate, collaborate and recreate.

SEASON DONORS

Founding Benefactor
The late Anthony Gilbert AM

Life Members
John Bell AO OBE
Tim Cox AO & Bryony Cox
Martin Dickson AM
& Susie Dickson
Virginia Henderson AM
David Pumphrey

Stage VI $50,000+
Atlas D□Aloisio Foundation
Tom & Elisabeth Karplus

Stage V $25,000+
John Hindmarsh AM
& Rosanna Hindmarsh OAM
Clear Pastoral Company
Ms Julia Ritchie
Mr Neil Sinden
& Mrs Rachel Sinden
Mr Alden Toevs &
Ms Judi Wolf

Stage IV $10,000+
Robert Albert AO
& Libby Albert
Susan Burns
Tim Cox AO & Bryony Cox
Anne & David Craig
Beau Deleuil
Martin Dickson AM
& Susie Dickson
Lachlan Edwards
Vic & Katie French
David Friedlander
Bill & Alison Hayward
Dr Gary Holmes
& Dr Anne Reeckmann
Dr Kimberly Cartwright
& Mr Charles Littrell
Ms Anne Loveridge
Mr Robert Maple-Brown AO
& Mrs Sue Maple-Brown AM
Brian & Helen McFadyen
Andrew Michael
Kenneth Reed AM
Sam Sheppard
Andrew Sisson

Stage III $5,000+
Peter Arthur
Ilana Atlas
& Tony D□Aloisio
John Bell AO OBE
& Anna Volska
Warwick & Lida Bray
Philip Chronican
Robert & Carmel Clark
Mrs Amy Crutchfield &
Mr Philip Crutchfield SC
Professor PJ Fletcher AM
Belinda Gibson
& Jim Murphy
Kathryn Greiner AO
Greg Hutchinson AM
& Lynda Hutchinson
Dr Sue Kesson
Michael Kingston
Marcus & Jessica
Laithwaite
Jill Morrison
David & Jill Pumphrey
Diane Sturrock
Gene Tilbrook
Dick & Sue Viney
Wesfarmers Arts
Sally White OAM
Janet Whiting AM
Anonymous (2)

Stage II $1,000+
Aesop
Bill & Kate Anderson
Mr Terrey Arcus AM
& Mrs Anne Arcus
Megan & David Armstrong
Australia-Britain
Society, Southern
Highlands Committee
Dr Margaret Barter
Helen Baxter
David & Annabelle
Bennett AO
Berg Family Foundation
Gail & Duncan Boyle
Graham Bradley AM
& Charlene Bradley
Dr John Brookes
Dr Catherine Brown-Watt
Bill & Sandra Burdett
Jan Burnswoods
John & Alison Cameron
John Cauchi AM SC
& Catherine Walker PSM
Yola & Steve Center
Jenny & Stephen Charles
Dr Diana Choquette
Kevin Cosgrave
Professor A T Craswell
Ms Patsy Crummer
Joanne & Sue Dalton
Darin Cooper Foundation
Antony de Jong
& Belinda Plotkin
Jane Diamond
Michael Diamond
John & Ros Dowling
Diane & John Dunlop
Dr & Mrs B Dutta
Elizabeth Evatt AC
Audette Exel
Ryissa Fogarty
Foxtel
David & Jo Frecker
Graham Froebel
Justin & Anne Gardener
Jennifer Giles
Sharon Goldschmidt
Louise Gourlay oam
Peter Graves
Mark & Patricia Grolman
Mark & Danielle Hadassin
Mr Peter Hall
Steven & Kristina Harvey
Catherine Parr
& Paul Hattaway
Jan Hayes
The Hon Peter Heerey AM QC
Jane Hemstritch
Linda Herd
In memory of
Armon Hicks Jnr
Michael Hobbs
Ken & Lilian Horler
Mike & Stephanie Hutchinson
Vincent Jewell
Cam & Caroline Johnston
Justice François Kunc QC
Julie & Michael Landvogt
Kate Lazar
Owen Lennie
Richard & Elizabeth Longes
Ms Danita Lowes
& Mr David Fite
Carolyn Lowry OAM
& Peter Lowry OAM
Hon Ian MacPhee AO
Maple-Brown Abbott Limited
Peter Mason AM & Kate Mason

BELL SHAKESPEARE DONORS CONT

Ms Ann McLaren
Alana Mitchell
In honour of Alden Toevs
Patricia Novikoff
Tom & Ruth O'Dea
Kathy Olsen & Bruce Flood
Rebel Penfold-Russell OAM
In memory of
Penelope Pether
Bob Richardson
Mr Andrew Roberts
Bridget & Peter Sack
Elisabeth & Doug Scott
Tim & Lynne Sherwood
Alan & Jenny Talbot
David & Jenny Templeman
Robert & Kyrenia Thomas
Mr Michael Thompson
C. Tooher
Mr Alexander White
George M Wilkins
Helen Williams AO
Frank Zipfinger
Anonymous (7)

Bequestor
Mr Irwin Imhof

In-Kind Supporters
Helen Bauer
Andy & Jill Griffiths
Donna St Clair

Bell Shakespeare would also like to thank our family of donors who have generously contributed up to $1000 – every gift makes a difference.

Sharing Shakespeare

Bell Shakespeare would like to thank our Sharing Shakespeare donors whose support provides those disadvantaged in our community with free or subsidised access to Hearts In A Row experiences, Actors At Work performances and Student Masterclass opportunities.

$10,000+
Robert Albert AO
& Libby Albert
Atlas D'Aloisio Foundation
Louise Christie
Martin Dickson AM
& Susie Dickson
John Hindmarsh AM
& Rosanna Hindmarsh OAM
Greg Hutchinson AM
& Lynda Hutchinson
Jane Hansen
& Paul Little AO
Ms Anne Loveridge
Nick & Caroline Minogue
Mrs Roslyn Packer AO
Annie & John Paterson Foundation
Stephen & Robbie Roberts
Wesfarmers Arts

$3,000+
Ilana Atlas
& Tony D'Aloisio
Graham Bradley AM
& Charlene Bradley
Christine Clough
Sally Collier
Kevin Cosgrave
Russ & Rae Cottle
Ms Amy Crutchfield &
Mr Philip Crutchfield QC
Richard England
Richard Evans
& Vanessa Duscio
David & Jo Frecker
Vic & Katie French
Kathryn Greiner AO
Mark & Danielle Hadassin
Joe Hayes
& Jacinta O'Meara
In memory of
Armon Hicks Jnr
Sofia Capodanno
& Hayden Hills
Julia & Nick Holder
Peter Jopling
Peter Los
Alexandra Martin
Sheila McGregor
Richard McHugh
The Pace Foundation
Rebel Penfold-Russell OAM
David & Jill Pumphrey

Rodney & Racquel Richardson
Ms Andreé Harkness
& Mr Richard Sewell
Sabrina Snow
Gene Tilbrook
David Watkins
Anonymous (2)

$1,500+
Paul Bedbrook
John Bell AO OBE
& Anna Volska
David & Annabelle Bennett
Catherine & Phillip Brenner
Elizabeth Bryan
John & Janet Calvert-Jones
Michelle Cameron
Jane Caro
Tim Cox AO & Bryony Cox
Graham Froebel
Tony & Chris Froggatt
Jinnie Gavin & Ross Gavin
Belinda Gibson
Deena Shiff
& Dr James Gillespie
Michael Happell
Meredith Hellicar
Linda Herd
Sally Herman
Susan E Horwitz
Julian Knights
Justice François Kunc QC
Ian Low
Jodie Lyons
Ian McGill
Deborah Page AM
Jim & Sally Peters
Beverley Price
Heather Ridout AO
Warren Scott
Deborah Thomas
Julie White
Helen Williams AO
Anonymous (2)

Bell Shakespeare also extend our deepest thanks to all Sharing Shakespeare donors who have generously contributed up to $1,500 – every gift enables us to educate and share the magic of live performance with those who would otherwise not have the opportunity.

BELL SHAKESPEARE BOARD, COMMITTEE + STAFF

Board of Directors
Ilana Atlas (Chairman)
Jane Caro
Philip Crutchfield QC
Peter Evans
Graham Froebel
Kathryn Greiner AO
Greg Hutchinson AM
Anne Loveridge
Gene Tilbrook
Alden Toevs
Janet Whiting AM
Helen Williams AO

Arts Advisory Committee
Jane Caro
Lyndsay Connors
Campion Decent
Peter Evans
Fran Kelly
Hugh Mackay AO
David Malouf AO

Artistic Director
Peter Evans

General Manager
Gill Perkins

Deputy General Manager
John Henderson

Executive Assistant
Imogen Gardam

Associate Director
James Evans

Writing Fellows
Jada Alberts
Kate Mulvany

Head of Operations
Patrick Buckle

Production Manager
Daniel Murtagh

Casting & Company Manager
Alex Souvlis

Assistant Company Manager
Eva Tandy

Technical Supervisor
Andrew Hutchinson

Personnel Manager
Susan Howard

Finance Manager
Jeanmaree Furtado

Bookkeeper
Sally Stevenson

Administrative Coordinator
Karina Kilpatrick

Head of Education
Joanna Erskine

Education Manager
Caitlin Brass

Education Coordinator
Michael Mitchell

Head of Marketing
Fiona Hulton

National Publicist
Jane Davis

Box Office Manager
Jesse Sturgeon

Marketing & Ticketing Coordinator
Justin Jefferys

Graphic Designer
Nathanael van der Reyden

Head of Development
Zoë Cobden-Jewitt

Corporate Development Manager
Amelia Lawrence

Major Gifts & Philanthropy Manager
Olivia Wynne

Development Executive
Kate Gardner

Development & Finance Coordinator
Laura Henderson

Campaign Design
Christopher Doyle & Co.

Media Agency
AKA

BELL SHAKESPEARE PARTNERS

Bell Shakespeare would like to thank the following:

Major Partner

National Schools Partner

Supporting Partner

Perth Season Partner

Company Partners

Accommodation Partner Melbourne

Special Event Partner

Accommodation Partner Canberra

Official Catering Partner Sydney

Printing Partner

Paper Partner

Accommodation Partner Sydney

Public Affairs Advisors

Legal Partner

Community Partner

Restaurant Partner Sydney

Media Partners

Government Partners

NSW Government Arts NSW

Australian Government Australia Council for the Arts

Bell Shakespeare Learning is supported by the Australian Government

Corporate Members

EY
JBWere
Lazard

Community Partners

Bill and Patricia Ritchie Foundation
Collier Charitable Fund
Crown Resorts Foundation
The Ian Potter Foundation
Intersticia Foundation
James N Kirby Foundation
The Limb Family Foundation
Packer Family Foundation Ltd
The Robert Salzer Foundation
The Rowley Foundation
Scully Fund
The Weir Anderson Foundation

www.currency.com.au

Visit Currency Press' website now to:

- Buy your books online
- Browse through our full list of titles, from plays to screenplays, books on theatre, film and music, and more
- Choose a play for your school or amateur performance group by cast size and gender
- Obtain information about performance rights
- Find out about theatre productions and other performing arts news across Australia
- For students, read our study guides
- For teachers, access syllabus and other relevant information
- Sign up for our email newsletter

The performing arts publisher

www.ingramcontent.com/pod-product-compliance
Lightning Source LLC
Chambersburg PA
CBHW050016090426
42734CB00021B/3294